Tactical Firearm

MW00882091

That you can use in the privacy of your own home to hardwire elite Spec Ops level combat and competition shooting skills quickly and for little to no money

by David Morris
and "Ox"

Skills demonstrated by "Top Shot" Season 3 Champion, Dustin Ellermann

Printed in USA
TacticalFirearmsTrainingSecrets.com
1930 Village Center Circle #3-1153
Las Vegas, NV 89134

Warning – Disclaimer

The information contained herein is the result of the authors' exhaustive study and research for their personal edification. Since individuals and situations vary, this information should be viewed solely for information purposes and applied with that in mind. You could die, get hurt, or end up in jail from applying the lessons in this book. Always get proper training and assistance from a qualified professional in your area before doing anything.

None of the parties involved in the production or distribution of this volume take, claim or accept any responsibility whatsoever for the use or misuse of the information contained herein regardless of motivation or intent.

Safety Warning!

Firearms are tools that give people the power to destroy at a distance. Firearms are inherently dangerous. Negligence and accidents can lead to permanent injuries, jail time, and possibly even death.

Treat every firearm as if it is loaded at all times, and don't point them at anything that you don't intend on destroying. Don't point them at a wall that may have something on the other side that you don't mind destroying. When you handle a firearm, YOU are responsible for everything that happens as a result, so get proper live training from a qualified instructor.

This book does not substitute for live training with a qualified instructor. It is meant to enhance and lock in the skills that you learn from live training. The author, publisher, editor, and talent for this book take no responsibility for what you do with firearms or what happens to you as a result of being around firearms.

If you don't think a particular activity is safe, or that you can safely do it, then don't do it.

Stay safe. Obey the law. Don't do careless things.

Sign up for additional firearms training for FREE!

As someone who has purchased this book, you are entitled to additional firearms training information for FREE by going to TacticalFirearmsTrainingSecrets.com/bonus.

While you're there, you'll be able to get additional training tips, interact with other shooters, and get priority notification about recommended training courses.

Table of Contents

Introduction

Thank you for buying this book. The book in your hands has the power to have the biggest impact on your shooting ability of any book you have ever read.

Why? Because it will help you get around the biggest obstacles to locking in and maintaining tactical firearms skills...time and money.

These tactics, techniques, and procedures are the very same ones that elite special operations units from around the globe, many with unlimited ammo budgets, use to train beginning and advanced tactics as well as maintain their edge.

Who else uses these tactics? Olympic athletes of all disciplines and competitive shooters, including the champion of Top Shot Season 3, Dustin Ellermannn, who you see on the cover and who graciously agreed to demonstrate the skills throughout.

Very special thanks to the named and unnamed shooters who contributed to this book in one way or another. A partial list has to include, Col. Randy Watt, 19SFG, Ethan MacAndrews, Rob Pincus, Michael Bane, Chris Wilden, Force Recon Marine, Brandonmichael Davis, Tim Schmidt, Robert Edan, Tim Larkin, T.T., Lt. Col, Army SF, K. Green, Rhadi Ferguson, and more. Some of you know how much you helped, others have no idea how much I appreciate you.

On another note, in addition to thanking him for his help with this book, I have to thank Dustin Ellermannn for being an awesome Christian role-model on Season 3 of Top Shot. My 4 year old son and I watched every week and my son would ask me almost every night if we could "watch Dustin shoot." It has been a pleasure to get to know Dustin and I want to encourage you to visit him at www.CampHisWay.com/topshot/bio

Firearms Accuracy

Chances are good that you or someone you know doesn't get to shoot as much as they'd like. In fact, as the cost of ammo has gone up and people have become more reluctant to shoot, it's not unusual to talk with people who have spent more on new guns in the last 12 months than they've spent on the ammo they've run through them!

Put that way, it sounds kind of silly, doesn't it? It may be silly, but it IS understandable. Let's say that you go out and buy a used Glock for $400 and you buy 1200 rounds of ammo to run through it for another $400. Spread that out over a year and it works out to 100 rounds a month...or just over $30.

Not too bad, but most people who shoot will quickly tell you that this is not the only cost. To begin with, it's very difficult for most people who love shooting to ONLY shoot 100 rounds per month. You've also got to add in range fees, targets, cleaning supplies, gas, and time. Time to drive to the range, time to shoot, time to drive home, and time to clean your firearm.

And I don't know about you, but every time I pull the trigger, there's a little cash register bell ringing in my head reminding me how much my outing is costing...and there are times when it rings a lot because I really enjoy shooting.

And, as I'm shooting and trying to keep my costs under control, I'm also trying to work on accuracy, my presentation, two handed, right hand, and left hand shooting, reloads, malfunctions, presentation from concealment, follow through, transitions between targets, stance, quickly acquiring my site picture, quickly reacquiring my site picture, short range shooting, long range shooting, one handed reloads, imagining scenarios, duck walking, cornering, low light, and more.

It's not easy to balance training 10-20 skills with the reality of time and money constraints, but that's exactly what we're going to talk about in this book.

You see, I've mined through thousands of pages of research, go through multiple advanced firearms classes every year, and have interviewed some of the best firearms instructors in the country (many would say the world) to unearth proven techniques for improving firearms skills as quickly as possible while spending as little money as possible. As I did more and more research and spoke with more and more "operators" and trainers, they finally got through to me that some of the most effective firearms training techniques available were inexpensive or even free.

The training techniques that I'm going to share with you have been proven over several decades by elite units such as the US Army Special Forces, US Navy Seals, Soviet and Russian Spetsnaz, GSG 9, British SAS, Detachment Delta & other SOCOM units, and Olympic gold medalists. They're used by professional and amateur competition shooters around the globe and, in many cases, they're the difference between first place and 5th or 6th place. Keep in mind that they don't use these techniques because of limited budgets—they use them because they're the absolute best training tools that they have available to them.

Self Defense, Politics, and Training

One of the specific applications of this training is going to be training to use a firearm for personal protection. That involves shooting while moving, around barriers, switching hands, and possibly drawing from concealment...actions that are frowned at on most ranges. I'll show you how you can still effectively train for these scenarios without having to go to great expense.

In addition, as various city, state, and federal agencies continue on their anti-gun paths, it's likely that it will become more and more expensive and difficult to train to defend yourself and your family with a firearm. I'll show you how you can continue training, no matter how oppressive things get.

Programming and Re-Programming Your Mind (Muscle Memory)

Working on the mental aspects of shooting isn't necessarily as fun as going out and blasting away at reactive targets, but it will help you become a better shooter in a shorter period of time.

In fact, it's important to realize that your firearm is not your real weapon. Your weapon is your mind. Your firearm simply allows you to use your weapon (your mind) to focus your strike with more force and at a longer distance than you can strike with your hands or feet. Your mind is truly the foundation for being able to quickly and accurately put rounds on target. Shooting with weak mental skills is like building a house of straw. Shooting with strong mental skills is like building a stone fortress on top of a mountain.

With that in mind, we're going to start with the mental aspects of shooting first.

A common saying among firearms trainers is that it takes 30005000 rounds to develop a new habit. Fortunately, this popular, often repeated number is specific enough that it's easy to find out where it came from. It comes from a textbook titled "Motor Learning and Performance" by Richard A. Schmidt that was published in 2004.

In it, what Schmidt actually says is that it takes 300-500 repetitions to develop a **new** motor skill and 3000-5000 repetitions to break a highly ingrained motor skill and replace it with a correct one. The good news is that if you have no ingrained skills or skills that have been practiced inconsistently, it will be easier to replace them with the skills you want to use when your life depends on it or even when you're just under extreme pressure to perform in a competitive situation.

Just to be clear, most people shoot inconsistently, so you'll PROBABLY be much closer to the 300-500 range than the 3000-5000 range—even if you've been shooting regularly for years.

The other side of this high repetition argument comes from Ed Head at Gunsite. There is common belief that shooting is a perishable skill that you need to continually train or risk losing it. Ed is a world class instructor and has a different take on shooting being a perishable skill. He maintains that you can turn a perishable skill like shooting into a locked-in reflex after approximately 3000-5000 rounds of training.

If you carry that logic out, you'd want to run through 5000 rounds with your primary hand, secondary hand, and with both hands with perfect form as quickly as possible. You'd also want to do it with your sidearm, long gun, and shotgun for an ammo count somewhere north of 35,000 rounds. It SOUNDS intimidating, but it doesn't have to be.

So, what's the trick to breaking old habits and locking in new ones so that they will be your default response when your life depends on it without breaking the bank?

Option 1: Join a SWAT unit or a Special Operations unit that gets paid to have LOTS of trigger time and free ammo.

Option 2: Become a professional shooter and get free ammo from your sponsor.

Option 3: "Cheat" by doing the majority of your training using low cost and free proven tactics that I'm going to share with you and using your live fire time to reinforce and lock in your skills. This shortcut method is not only the fastest possible way for you to become an expert shot with a firearm, it will also save you thousands of dollars and years of time in the process.

So let's get started. We're going to quickly cover some fundamentals and then we'll move into the actual strategies. I will be primarily using pistols for the examples, but the techniques will work with pistols, revolvers, rifles, and shotguns. The techniques will also work with whatever particular shooting style you have learned.

That being said, you'd better be VERY confident that your technique is the one that you want to learn, because after going through this series, that technique will be imprinted deeply in your subconscious mind and it will become your new "default" when you need to operate under stress.

There are 5 factors that will determine just how quickly your skill improves and how locked in the skills become:

1. **The quality of the technique you practice.** The old saying, "Garbage In Garbage Out" applies. If you practice bad technique enough times, you'll revert to it when you're under stress. If, on the other hand, you focus on practicing good technique, your default response under stress will be much better.

2. **The consistency of the technique.** I'm going to refer to this example frequently, so you might want to read it twice. I want you to envision two quarterbacks throwing 100 passes. The first quarterback focuses on speed and how fast he can get through his 100 throws. He ends up changing something with every throw... his stance, his balance, his grip, what he does with his off hand, the angle of his body to the target, his release, and his follow-through, etc. In looking at his 100 passes, you see that he threw 100 different ways...but he did it really fast. Impressively fast.

The second quarterback takes his time and focuses on doing absolutely everything the same with every throw so that, at the end of 100 passes, the video looks like the same footage spliced end-to-end 100 times. (or 99 times for you fellow geeks reading this)

At the end of the 100 throws, whose mind do you think has a more ingrained image of what a perfect throw feels like? Who do you think has developed more consistent muscle memory? Which one of them has a more solid base to unconsciously revert to under stress when there's barely enough time to react?

This second quarterback is the model that we want to copy by deciding on proper technique and using it every single time you practice. When the first quarterback's mind gets under stress and trys to throw a pass, it's going to be confused and it won't know which muscle sequence to fire.

3. Number of repetitions

4. **Frequency of training**: If you have the option of doing 5000 repetitions over one month or one year, you'll lock in the technique better if you do the repetitions in as little time as possible without sacrificing quality. While it's important to get the repetitions done quickly, the goal isn't to blast through them...the goal is to imprint perfect technique into your subconscious mind. That being said, remember to stop your practice sessions as soon

as you're no longer able to execute the skills you're practicing with perfect form.

5. **Speed of training:** One of the experts that I consulted for this, Tim Larkin, had a career in Naval Intelligence and went through BUD/S (SEAL) training. Near the end of the training, he had a catastrophic eardrum rupture that prevented him from wearing the Trident. He told me about how SEALs were taught high speed firearms skills.

    Surprisingly, they weren't given live ammo for the first two weeks. All they did was draw an empty firearm from their holster, aim it at their target, and squeeze until they heard the gun go "click." Then, they'd rack the slide, re-holster, and repeat. And repeat. And repeat. As Tim said, he'd been shooting all of his life, and felt like he was being treated like a child rather than the expert that he already was.

    To make it worse, they made him go S L O W. And they made him do it perfectly every time. By the time they actually gave him ammo, he'd dry fired thousands of times...and he'd ingrained perfect technique deeply into his mind. His mind knew the exact sequence of micro movements necessary to perform a perfect shot and his mind was able to fire the sequence at any speed... slow OR fast.

    This is the interesting part about how the training played out. The mind remembers the specific sequence of muscles to fire without remembering the speed. Saying it in a slightly different way, that means that once a technique is locked in by training at slow speed, it can be used at high speed under stress.

    Back to the football example, if he would have trained fast, he would have had dozens, perhaps hundreds of sequences that his brain could have played back, leading to inconsistent results. But since he went slowly and focused on consistency, the sequence that he played back was the same every time.

Quality, Consistency, Volume, Frequency & Speed. Remember them. They're going to be the keys to the kingdom of firearms accuracy.

A quick word on safety.

No article, book, or course on firearms training would be complete without the attorney mandated warning not to do stupid things that hurt people. Specifically,

1. ALWAYS keep your firearm pointed in a safe direction.

2. ALWAYS keep your finger off the trigger until you're ready to shoot.

3. ALWAYS keep your firearm unloaded until ready to use.

Keep in mind that these apply whether you're using a firearm that shoots bullets, BBs, lasers, or anything else.

Two force multipliers that will shorten your training cycle even more.

In one of my interviews with Colonel Randy Watt of the 19th Special Forces Group, we discussed a study that was done by The University of Miami at Ohio. In it, they attempted to identify things that they could test on people to predict how well they would be able to perform with a firearm.

Two of the biggest factors that they identified were grip strength and overall fitness. Above a certain point, grip strength does not continue to improve firearms accuracy, but if you have weak grip strength, strengthening it to where you have average to above average grip strength will have a dramatic positive effect on your accuracy.

Overall fitness is particularly important for people who carry their excess weight above the belt. The reason is simple physics. A proper shooting stance is an aggressive stance with the upper body slanted towards the direction of fire. Any extra belly weight ends up being out in front of the hips, pulling against the spine, either causing lower back fatigue or lower back pain when the muscles can no longer compensate for the weight.

This is one reason why it's normal to see overweight shooters standing straight up at the range and then leaning backwards as they slowly lose the battle against recoil on multiple shot drills.

This doesn't mean that you can't improve your firearms speed and accuracy if you have a weak grip and are overweight. I've been outshot by guys who are literally twice as heavy as I am in competition because they have made tremendous efforts to compensate for their weight. But for most people who are serious about improving their shooting; fitness and grip strength are force multipliers that can't be ignored.

It's similar to hikers who will trim the laces on their shoes, cut all of the labels off of their gear, and cut their toothbrushes in half to cut weight but carry an extra 10-15 pounds around the waist. All of those little steps WILL help some, but making the fundamental step of losing the extra weight can cause a quantum leap in performance.

How to develop high quality speed.

Speed is important in firearms training. Whether it is clearing a cover garment, getting a consistent grip, clearing the holster, acquiring the sights, or squeezing off the first and subsequent rounds, speed is crucial.

But there are different qualities of speed. I touched on this earlier with the story of the two quarterbacks and with Tim Larkin's BUD/S training, but the key to developing high quality speed is to repeatedly practice a given technique exactly the same way.

Another mental picture is using a cable saw to cut through a log. If you reposition your saw after every stroke, you will end up with lots of shallow cuts on the log, but no progress towards cutting through it. Running the cable saw over the exact same spot as few as a dozen times, on the other hand, will work a permanent groove into the log and eventually cut through it. It's probably pretty evident by now that repeatedly working the exact same groove with the cable saw is the same as working the exact same technique with your firearm. It will help you get the results you're looking for MUCH faster than inconsistent technique.

The trick to repeatedly performing a technique EXACTLY the same way

The most powerful trick for practicing consistent technique is to do the technique slowly. Frankly, I don't like slow. I like FAST. I like doing things quickly, learning quickly, and blasting through obstacles quickly. Ironically, training slowly is going to increase your default speed quicker than training fast!

I remember going shooting with my brother after he'd just gotten back from leading a SF team in Afghanistan. I started shooting and I was trying to get off double taps from concealment as quickly as possible.

When he started shooting, he looked like a turtle crawling through molasses. But he had absolutely no wasted movement and every shot was identical. As he sped up, he kept the same efficiency and consistency, and was quickly shooting faster and more accurately than me.

You've heard the saying, "Slow is smooth and smooth is fast" and there's a reason for that:

- Smooth movement is efficient and doesn't waste motion. -If you repeat smooth movement consistently in slow motion, it will wear a groove in the brain and your default movement will be smooth and efficient.

- Just like the shortest distance between two points is a straight line, the fastest technique is the one that is the smoothest and wastes the least motion.

- When you are under stress and acting quickly, your brain will quickly playback whatever groove is worn the deepest. If that groove happens to be a smooth, efficient technique, then you will perform smooth and efficiently under stress.

When you are training techniques, especially initially, you want your technique to look the same as a competition shooter looks at $\frac{1}{2}$ or $\frac{1}{4}$ speed. Said another way, if you were to videotape yourself, you should be able to play it back at 2x or 4x speed and have it look like a competition shooter...perfect, smooth, and free of wasted motion.

Where does recoil make you pivot?

This may seem like an odd question, but it's vital to consistent firearms performance...especially when firing multiple shots.

When someone fires a handgun with a loose wrist, it's called limp wristing and it can cause a failure to feed the next round. This is because the recoil is causing a rotation at the wrist. If you tighten the wrist, the next joint where you can rotate is the elbow. Tighten the elbow and the next joint to rotate is the shoulder. An example of rotating around the shoulder is when a shooter shoots a handgun, only to have it end up pointing straight up in the air when they're done.

Once you tighten the shoulder, the next joint to rotate is the waist. It's common to see new shooters with their hips thrown forwards and their shoulders thrown back a little bit further after every shot if they don't know that they should have a forward leaning, aggressive stance...kind of like a fighter in mid punch.

But if you tighten your wrist, elbow, shoulder, and waist and have a fighting stance with your spine bent slightly forward, you end up rotating around your front foot and your back foot acts like a break, stabilizing you and helping you keep a solid shooting platform so you can get off subsequent shots without having to make major aiming adjustments.

One of the big reasons that this works so well is that when your wrist, elbow, shoulder, and waist are flexed, the recoil of the shot gets absorbed by the mass of your entire body, rather than just your hand, arm, or upper body (*figure 1*).

(*figure 1*)

I'll get into detail on specific techniques and strategies in the next section, but for right now, let's talk about some concrete steps that you can take over the next few days & weeks to put this information to use.

1. Pick one firearm to start practicing these skills with. "Muscle confusion" is a sexy technique for fitness, but not something that you want to do with firearms training.

2. Take at least half of your dry fire and range time this month and spend it trying to do everything at 10-20 percent of full speed. Focus on removing any unnecessary movement from your draw stroke and make sure that you are using the exact same technique every time.

3. As you're returning your firearm to your holster, don't think of it as holstering your firearm. Think of it as drawing your firearm

in reverse and try to do everything in the exact opposite order that you did when you drew your firearm. (You're going to have to determine if you can do this safely at the range.) This is not necessarily the best way to re-holster your firearm. It is simply a way to "work the groove" of your muscle memory in both directions. In the pictures below, Dustin is showing a sample sequence of grip, clear, high ready, and full extension (*figure 2*). If any of this is new, we'll go into it more in a little bit.

(*figure 2*)

4. During your dry fire time, practice drawing your firearm while facing a mirror. If you have a video camera available, record yourself a few times, watch, analyze, fix, and repeat. Focus on getting rid of inefficiencies and smoothness. If possible, try watching the video at 2x or even 4x speed and see how it looks— it should look the way you want to perform under stress.

In the coming sections, we'll go over specific techniques and tools that you can use to make your learning curve almost vertical, as well as training sequences and exercises.

For questions and additional information, please go to
TacticalFirearmsTrainingSecrets.com/bonus

Dry Fire

Technique #1: Dry Fire...The Fastest Way To Lock in Firearms Skill:

Dry fire is one of those topics that people like to talk about, but few actually do. I can understand that...I don't find it to be particularly exciting, and it's kind of frustrating only going through the motions with a firearm when I know how much fun it is to actually shoot.

But the benefits of dry fire are overwhelming...and if you really want to become proficient with your firearm, it's important to understand that a combination of dry fire and live fire will help you improve much quicker and cheaper than live fire alone.

If you're a fan of boxing or MMA, one of the most relatable ways to look at dry fire training is to realize that it is shooting version of shadow boxing. Many professional boxers "shadow" throw the 9 basic punches 1,000 times per day, for a total of 9,000 shadow punches every day—perfecting their technique, timing, efficiency, muscle memory, and speed without undue stress on their body. Dry fire will give you the same benefits.

In addition, dry fire training will almost guarantee that you don't fall victim to the most common handgun shooting error—jerking the firearm in anticipation of recoil.

Not everyone's like me and some people DO want to practice dry fire techniques, but they still don't get it done because they don't have a clear action plan of what to do when they are doing their dry fire training. It becomes easier to just put off dry fire training until tomorrow instead of figuring out exactly what drills to do. We'll cover that, too.

Dry fire training will help you focus on all of the fundamentals shooting... right up until the firing pin hits the primer. And it will allow you to focus on all of these fundamentals without paying for ammo, range time, gas, or having to clean your firearm. From a teaching perspective, it programs your mind without any concern for recoil and the downward flinch and low groups that come from anticipating recoil.

We're mainly going to cover fundamentals in this section, but I'm also going to show you some of the drills that I use that will REALLY spice up your dry fire drills. But first we need to lay a solid foundation and go over how to properly practice dry fire as well as some specific drills you can do to help you lock in good, fundamental shooting techniques.

If you want to know how much you should practice dry firing, a good rule of thumb is that you should dry fire 20 to 50 times for every round that you practice live fire. It would be great if you could practice every technique 1,000 times per day like a professional fighter, but that's not realistic for most people.

Still, try to do as many as your schedule allows. The one major exception to this is that you should slow down or stop as soon as your form falls off. Doing dry fire training with poor or inconsistent form will only hurt your ability to develop high quality muscle memory. Remember, we want to lock PERFECT technique into our muscle memory...not a combination of 80% perfect training and 20% sloppy training.

The high ratio of dry fire to live fire is most important during the learning phase. The logic behind it is based in part on the fact that when you train with live fire, any misses are a waste of time, money, and muscle memory. Once you've got the muscle memory locked in with dry fire, you can spend more time on live fire training because you won't be wasting time, money, or muscle memory.

The other part of why you want to spend so much time locking in and perfecting techniques with dry fire is because it allows you to completely ignore the "boom" and recoil and focus on proper technique. Breaking down the process like this will help you get many more rounds on target, more quickly, than with live fire alone.

Since we're dealing with a firearm designed to cause lethal damage, I've got to tell you the obvious advice of making sure that your firearm is unloaded when you're handling it and that you don't point it at anything you don't intend on destroying. I don't mean for this to be a downer, but anything having to do with a firearm, ESPECIALLY dry fire training, is serious business.

I said this before, but it's worth repeating. The general concepts behind these drills will work for ANY type of firearm...pistol, revolver, shotgun, rifle and any type of action...single, double, DAO, pump, break, bolt, semi-auto, etc. Because of popularity and for ease of reading, I'm going to focus on semi-automatic pistols. If you're not training with a semi-automatic pistol, please adjust the following rules accordingly.

Safety RULES (not guidelines or suggestions...they're RULES.)

1. Get rid of all distractions, electronic, 2 legged, and 4 legged, while you're training and make sure that your mental state is un-altered, clear, well rested, and that you are able to safely manipulate a firearm.

2. Make sure to remove the magazine, fully rack the slide 3 times, lock the slide open, visually inspect the chamber and physically inspect the chamber by inserting a finger to confirm that your weapon doesn't have any ammo in it. In the pictures below, Dustin shows what you should see when you visually inspect a pistol, how you should physically inspect a pistol, and how you should properly hand it off so that they can verify that it is empty (*figure 3*).

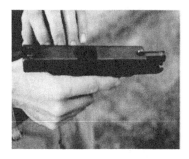

(*figure 3*)

3. Remove any live ammo from the room where you're doing dry fire training. If you use dummy rounds, empty them from your magazines until you can see the follower on every magazine you intend to use and can confirm that they're empty.

4. Pick a backstop that will stop any negligent discharges. Another way of looking at this is to quickly calculate the cost of a negligent discharge and decide if you could live with it. For me, when I do dry fire training at home, this means that I do my dry fire in our basement facing an outside wall so that the most likely outcome of a negligent discharge would be some sheetrock repair, possibly

bracing a damaged (non load bearing) stud, possibly replacing a section of wiring, and a slight chance of ricochet damage.

5. Always treat your firearm as if it's loaded—even during dry fire training. This means using proper gun handling discipline at all times. All of my friends who have had negligent discharges have had them with "empty" firearms.

6. Always know what's beyond your target and backstop.

7. Never point your gun at anything you're not willing to destroy—and that goes for TVs, people in the next room, next door neighbors, cars, etc. This is serious business and your first and only negligent action could kill someone, ruin your life, and possibly put you in jail. As mentioned in rule #4, calculate the potential cost.

8. The transition from dry fire back to live ammo is a particularly critical time.

   When you finish your dry fire training, the first step you should take is to take down the target that you used. According to the instructors at FrontSight, practicing "just one more time" is one of the most common reasons that dry fire training negligent discharges happen. Removing your dry fire target is one more way to insure safety.

   When you re-introduce live ammo, repeat the following phrase out loud until your firearm is holstered or stored securely, "Live ammo, Live weapon. Live ammo, Live weapon." It's important that you say these words out loud the entire time you're handling your firearm when you're transitioning from dry fire to live ammo.

   The transition from dry fire to live ammo is so critical that some trainers even suggest storing the weapon that you are doing dry fire training with for a half hour or more before re-introducing live ammo.

As an additional safety measure, you can run a piece of paracord through the barrel so that it sticks out of both the muzzle and ejection port, use a snap cap, or a Blade-Tech training barrel insert, or even a dedicated SIRT training pistol. **None of these are a replacement for the rules above. They should be used in addition, not instead of the above rules.**

Too much fuss over safety? This is serious business. You're training with a tool that's designed to destroy things at a distance. I oftentimes say that ALL of my friends who have had negligent discharges during dry fire or cleaning had them with firearms that they THOUGHT were empty. If you aren't completely confident about having the discipline to follow the rules above perfectly, then have a firearms instructor work with you until you are.

Now that we've got that covered, let's start training!

Consistent Grip. Having a consistent grip is the foundation of shooting. I believe it was famed firearms instructor, Colonel Jeff Cooper who said that if he had an hour to spend training someone with a pistol, he'd spend 50 minutes of that hour teaching them how to consistently obtain a proper grip.

After going through the safety steps I mentioned, grab the firearm that you want to start training with and take a couple of minutes to REALLY pay attention to how it feels in your hand(s). Take note of how every square inch of your hand feels and what it's touching. You don't even need your firearm in your holster right now. Just hold it in your hand(s) using whatever technique you have been taught or adopted.

This may seem kind of "touchy feely", but if you're training for the possibility of using a firearm to defend yourself in a lethal force encounter, it makes sense that you take the time to "get to know it."

In general, I'd tell you that you want to have a "natural" grip on the firearm. Here's an example of what your natural grip would be when firing one handed.

1. Bring your hands up to your face and make two fists, like a boxer.

2. Pick a target to punch.

3. Very slowly, go through the motions of throwing a punch with your shooting arm. Stop the punch when your arm is outstretched

and is perpendicular to your body (makes an "L"). Rotate your fist so that if you were holding a pencil or broom, it would be at a 45 degree angle to the ground. Note how in the picture below, Dustin's fist is naturally rotated as if he was throwing a punch and the magazine in his hand is lined up with his eye (*figure 4*).

(*figure 4*)

If you were to release your fist, put your firearm in your hand, and make your fist around the firearm so that your sights are lined up with your target, you'd have your natural one handed grip. By rotating your hand so that if you were holding a pencil or broom it would be straight up and down and bringing it together with your support hand, you'll roughly have your natural two handed grip (*figure 5*).

(figure 5)

Instructors differ on the nuances on the best grips, so I'll simply encourage you to get competent instruction and train what they teach you. I've done formal training with numerous Spec Ops guys, local and federal SWAT operators, mercenaries/security contractors, and one notable champion speed shooter and their techniques are all slightly different based on their experiences and biases. In their common quest for efficiency and effectiveness, most of them have ended up with VERY similar techniques based on getting the most "meat on metal" as possible, so don't get too hung up on minor differences from one instructor to another.

Your grip will be slightly different from firearm to firearm. My grip is different with my Glocks, 1911s, and with my revolvers. Grip angle is different, the girth of the grip is different, and the shape is different, varying from a square with Glocks to a rectangle with 1911s to an oval with revolvers. That being said, my grip on my Glocks is exactly the same every time. I know the feel of the grip against my hand and I know when it's off slightly without looking. The reason I'm able to do this is that I took the time, several times, to consciously pay attention to how the firearm feels in my hand(s).

I pay attention to what each joint of each finger is touching and how it feels. I pay attention to the pressure on the webbing between my thumb and index finger. I know how far forward the thumb on my shooting hand goes and

www.TacticalFirearmsTrainingSecrets.com

what it is touching. I know where my index finger will touch the trigger and I know what the side of the gun feels like when my finger is off the trigger.

On my subcompact, I know that my pinky slides under the grip with my subcompact mags and touches the front of the mag on full size mags.

As you're holding your firearm, take a minute to identify these same specific feelings on your firearm.

Now move your hand slightly, figure out what's different and what you will do to fix the situation if you feel the same in the future.

As an example, if you grab your firearm, the webbing between your thumb and index finger should be as high up on the grip as possible. If you recognize that you don't have the right pressure against your webbing, you know that you need to move your grip up on the pistol.

As another example, I know that when I grab a 1911, my first knuckles are all straight in front of the front strap and I know how that feels. If my hand is wrapped around the grip too much or not enough, I know what I need to do without looking to correct my grip.

Besides acquiring a bad grip during your draw stroke, one of the most common corrections that you'll need to make if you've got shorter fingers is during the process of reloading. On a semi auto with a thumb side mag release, most people can't touch the mag release button with their thumb when they have a proper grip on the firearm.

To fix this problem, people generally "cant" their firearm or rotate it in their grip so that their thumb can reach the mag release button. At some point between when you depress the mag release button and when you get ready for your next shot, you're going to need to reacquire a proper grip. Most people do this without thinking and have poor muzzle discipline during the procedure. I want you to focus on making these changes in your grip while maintaining proper muzzle discipline.

Take a couple of minutes and move the gun back and forth between a good grip and a grip that needs to be fixed. Make sure that you maintain proper muzzle discipline. Specifically, work on your response when you find yourself grabbing the firearm in the following ways:

1. Too low of a grip.

2. Too high of a grip.

3. Web of your hand away from the grip.

4. Bottom of your grip away from the butt of the grip.

Two handed grip with your support thumb wrapped around the grip on top of your shooting thumb (*figure 6*). (Leads to a "snakebite" or two slices across the top of your support thumb when your slide flies back during recoil.) This may work well for revolvers, but you'll want to avoid it like the plague with semi-autos.

(figure 6)

1. Firearm turned too far clockwise.

2. Firearm turned too far counterclockwise.

After you have gotten comfortable with the difference between the feel of a good grip and a bad grip, grab your firearm a few times while looking at it and then look away or with your eyes shut. Finally, following the dry fire safety rules, lay your firearm down on a table or the ground within arm's reach, shut your eyes, grab it and pick it up 20 times in a row. Each time you pick it up, evaluate whether or not you are holding it correctly. If not, identify what's wrong and adjust it until it feels perfect, open your eyes to confirm, then set it back down.

This may seem like an unnecessary exercise, but it is critical to expose your mind/body to as many problems as possible so that it can identify and respond to those problems without thinking or with minimal thought in low light, high stress, tunnel vision, or other sub-optimal conditions.

You'll want to get similarly familiar with any weapons that you might use for self-defense. For now, let your brain focus on training with one particular firearm until the grooves in your memory are worn deep.

Trigger Press

The next skill we're going to go over is a smooth trigger pull/press. Visually and physically confirm (again) that the firearm is unloaded. Then bring the empty firearm up and aim it at something you don't mind destroying and slowly pull the trigger straight back...the smaller and more precise the target, the better. Your trigger finger shouldn't squeeze like you're making a fist or push off to the side—It should press straight back. You should keep aiming as you pull the trigger and your aim should never come off of the intended target, even when the trigger breaks and the firing pin is released to strike the primer on your bullet. You should press the trigger slowly enough that you don't know when the release will happen.

As you continue to practice keeping your sights lined up all the way through the trigger press, you'll be able to speed up your trigger press without any impact on your accuracy. In general, don't press the trigger so fast that your sight alignment gets messed up, but keep trying to squeeze the trigger faster.

Re-rack the slide on your firearm between dry fires (while maintaining muzzle discipline) and practice your trigger press 10 times. Specifically, you're trying to condition your mind to do three things with this drill: Aim all the way through the trigger press. Squeeze the trigger instead of jerking it. Keep the firearm aimed at your intended target instead of trying to compensate for recoil by pushing the point of aim down.

While practicing this, it's very common to notice something that you never noticed while shooting live fire—a sticky or jerky trigger. This can make a smooth trigger press much more difficult, and it is a good sign that you need to clean and lubricate your firearm.

Do repeat sets of 10 until you can keep your sights on target all the way through your trigger press for all 10 repetitions, then try this fun training technique:

Pick a target that is roughly at the same height as your eyes, aim at it with your firearm and lay a coin on the front sight (this may not be possible on all pistols) and pull the trigger. Your trigger squeeze should be so smooth that the coin stays on the front sight and doesn't fall off as you're squeezing the trigger (*figure 7*). The release of the hammer may vibrate the coin off. That's out of your control and OK.

(*figure 7*)

Follow through. Now we're going to add on follow through. This is as important with shooting as it is with basketball, golf, baseball, and other physical activities. As you're dry firing, think about getting a proper sight picture, firing, and then following through by getting the proper sight picture again as quickly as possible. You won't have recoil to worry about when dry firing, so your sight picture should stay constant, but this is a good time to repeat the refrain, "sight picture, trigger press, sight picture."

If you're fuzzy on what a "sight picture" is, it's what you see as you're looking at a target when you have your firearm lined up for a perfect shot. Generally, this means having the front sight perfectly centered between the rear sights, front and rear sights lined up vertically, and the intended target immediately over the top of the front sight.

Practice dry firing 10 times focusing on reacquiring your sights immediately after the trigger breaks.

Repeat this drill until you can quickly reacquire your sights after pressing the trigger, then move on.

Trigger reset. After you discharge a firearm, the trigger only needs to go forward until the seer re-engages for the next shot. On double action pistols, this may be $^1/_2$ the distance that your finger traveled for the first shot, or less. If your trigger or your finger travels further forward after a shot than the point where the seer re-engages, it's called "over travel" and it's not good.

Over travel leads to inconsistent follow-up shots. From now on, unless you're shooting the last repetition of a set, every time you dry fire, keep the trigger pressed until you have racked the slide. Then slowly let the trigger go forward until you feel/hear the click of the seer re-engaging and immediately press for your next shot. Mastering trigger reset is absolutely VITAL to being able to put multiple rounds on target quickly and your sequence will become:

Sight picture, trigger press, sight picture (follow through), trigger reset, trigger press

The combination of follow-through and trigger reset will help you get on target MUCH faster for controlled pairs and other multiple shot strings.

Practice dry firing 20 times, putting together the entire sequence. Go only as fast as you can without compromising your form:

Sight picture, trigger press, sight picture, trigger reset, trigger press

Bringing your firearm up into your line of sight.

You should practice this drill using both one and two hands.

When you can pull the trigger smoothly and consistently, it's time to move on. When you're shooting at a range, you'll see people go through all sorts of contortions with their heads while they're shooting trying to get their eye lined up with the sights on their firearms.

In a violent force encounter, your focus will normally be drawn to what your brain interprets as the most serious threat. In addition, as your pulse rate shoots up, your vision will go from being able to see everything in front of you to tunnel vision— similar to what it would look like if you held an empty paper towel cylinder up to your eye.

We want to take advantage of this tendency instead of trying to fight it, so we want to train our mind to bring our firearm up so that our sights will be in our line of sight rather than forcing our head and eyes to line up with our sights (*figure 8*).

(*figure 8*)

Put another way, let's say that you're holding your firearm at your side and you spot a target. At this point, your head can freeze. You don't need to move your head at all from the instant of threat recognition until you have completed your trigger press and follow through. Simply bring up your firearm and adjust the firearm as necessary so that your sights are in line between your eyes and your intended target. You're already familiar with this concept from using a punching motion to find your natural grip.

What you need to do to develop this is to stand with your firearm at your side or sit with your firearm on your lap or on a table and repeatedly pick out a target and bring your firearm up so that the sights line up between your eye and your target.

There are 4 variations to this drill:

Primary hand, single handed
Primary hand, with support
Support hand, single handed
Support hand, with support

Repeat this drill at least 20 times with your primary hand both single handed and with support before moving on. Initially, either focus completely on your primary hand or spend twice as much time on your primary hand as your support hand. In an ideal world, you would have enough time to become equally proficient with both hands. If that's the case for you, then split your training time evenly.

Aiming With Your Eyes Shut.

You should do this drill using one or two hands.

This drill helps strengthen the mind-muscle connection to lock in your natural point of aim so that it's the same as the point where you're focusing your eyes.

With your firearm at your side, look at the target that you were using on the last drill. Now, shut your eyes, bring up your firearm until you think it is aiming at your target and open your eyes to confirm. Adjust your firearm as necessary so that it's aimed correctly and take note of how everything feels and repeat the drill.

You'll find that this is much easier if you keep your firearm close to your body as you raise it up to your chest in a "high ready" or "high compressed ready" position and "punch" it straight out rather than swinging it up in an arc. There are a couple of tactically sound reasons for this. First, when you swing, there is a tendency to over-swing , which wastes time and decreases accuracy. Second, if you train to begin aiming at your target from the time you're in a high compressed ready position until your firearm is extended and your sights are lined up, it's possible to take combat accurate shots much quicker than if you swing your pistol into position. (We'll cover this concept more in a moment) Not surprisingly, this is also the most "efficient" way to raise a firearm and the method used by people who regularly use firearms in lethal force encounters.

This drill may take a few sessions to master, but once you do, you'll notice a dramatic improvement in your ability to engage targets quickly.

Dustin illustrates this sequence in this set of photos that I shared with you earlier (*figure 9*):

(*figure 9*)

This particular drill is very valuable for several reasons. The first of which is that you may find your sights broken or obscured at some point when you NEED to fire. If you know that your natural point of aim will put rounds on target, you will be less likely to hesitate.

Second, despite repeatedly training to aim with their sights, there are numerous stories of law enforcement who shot attackers and don't remember seeing their sights...they only remember seeing the barrel of the gun pointed at them by an attacker and the biggest fire they've ever seen coming out of the end, and firing back. By training so that when you raise your weapon, your sights naturally come into alignment with your eyes and your target, you're more likely to be able to put rounds on target under extreme stress.

From a self defense standpoint, there's an even more important reason for training bringing your firearm up to your line of sight rather than moving your eyes so they line up with your firearm.

In "Sharpening the Warrior's Edge" Bruce Siddle goes into detail about how your ability to focus on close up objects diminishes with high pulse rates induced by stress. Focusing the eye is a function of the parasympathetic nervous system and it works very well normally. Once stress levels and pulse rates go up, your body switches over to the sympathetic nervous system. This happens somewhere between 145 and 175 beats per second. Unfortunately, the sympathetic nervous system isn't very good at details like focusing on objects close to you...like your sights.

So, if you practice bringing your firearm up into your line of sight and train to find your natural point of aim, you'll be much more likely to be able to get off accurate shots under extreme stress when you may or may not be able to focus. This is important, both because you want to be able to stop violent threats as efficiently as possible and because you are responsible for every round that you fire.

There are 4 variations to this drill:

Primary hand, single handed
Primary hand, with support
Support hand, single handed
Support hand, with support

Repeat this drill at least 20 times with your primary hand both single handed and with support before moving on.

3 "Position" Draw Stroke

This draw stroke is sometimes called the 3 position draw stroke, 4 position draw stroke, 3 part drawstroke, or 4 part drawstroke. The confusion comes from the fact that there are different naming systems for the same draw-stroke.

1. **"Holster"** -- Firearm holstered, hand off of the firearm.

2. **"Grip"** – Firearm holstered, correct grip on firearm (*figure 10*).

(*figure 10*)

3. **"Position 1"** – Firearm just clearing the holster (*figure 11*).

(*figure 11*)

4. **"Position 2"** – Body square to your target, firearm at chest level, tilted outward with the butt of the firearm against your chest.

This is where you disengage and reengage your safety, if you have one.

Without a firearm in your hand, you would be making a fist with your palm up against the side of your chest like you would if you were preparing to throw a "formal" martial arts punch. If you were to fire the firearm from this position, the slide would not hit your chest like it would if the firearm was straight up and down. Conceptually, you should have your firearm aimed at your target from this point on, so that you can fire at any time and make solid hits on your target.

(figure 12)

There is debate on what to do with your support hand at this step. The two big schools of thought are 1. To grab the center of your shirt like in the two photos above (*figure 12*) and pull or 2. Friend and famed tactical firearms instructor, Rob Pincus of ICE Training teaches students to hold your support hand up near your face in a defensive position (*figure 13*), since it's likely that you'll be drawing after being startled and that's where your hand will go during a normal startle response anyhow.

(figure 13)

5. **"Position 3"** – Firearm is pushed out into firing position with the sights on your firearm coming into alignment between your eyes and your target. The motion from Position 2 to Position 3 is a simple punch, with your firearm remaining aimed at your target throughout the entire motion.

There's also debate on whether to hold your support hand in front of your chest to "catch" your firearm as it's moving forward or to have it follow behind and "catchup" between position 2 and position 3. Personally, I am a fan of "catching up" or just shooting one handed, but the experts that I've trained under are split down the middle on which technique is better.

In general, if you are in a situation where you are in control of your pulse, such as in competition or a combat veteran, it's better to use 2 hands and the "catch" method will allow you to put rounds on target more accurately and quickly. If, on the other hand, you're training to defend yourself in what will be your first—or one of your first—lethal force encounters, you're better off training to "catch up" to minimize the chance of shooting your support hand.

Practice going through the following sequence 10 times using only your strong hand:

Holster, Grip, Position 1, Position 2, Holster -- Pay attention to your grip, that your firearm is pointed towards your target in position 2, and that you can holster your firearm without looking at your holster.

We're starting to stack multiple muscle sequences on top of one another and it's VITAL that you only go fast enough that you can repeat these techniques smoothly, efficiently, and exactly the same way every time. If you're getting flustered or messing up, S L O W down. You'll develop speed more quickly by becoming efficient than you will by moving fast.

Repeat if you're not smooth and efficient, otherwise, go through the following sequence 10 times using only your strong hand:

Holster, Grip, Position 2, Safety off, Position 3, Position 2, Safety on, Holster

Repeat if you're not smooth and efficient, otherwise go through the following sequence 10 times using only your strong hand:

Holster, Grip, Position 2, Safety off, Position 3, Trigger press, Rack the slide, Position 2, Safety on, Holster

Variations on this that you'll want to practice are:

Strong hand only.

Strong hand with support.

Support hand only. (I don't practice drawing with my support hand and then using a 2 handed grip because I would use my strong hand to draw unless it was injured. If it was injured, it's not likely that I could use it for support.)

Drawing From Concealment

You may be fortunate, like me, to have a range that allows you to draw from concealment. As they've gotten to know me and my gun handling discipline, they'll even put me on an end lane and let me use an ankle holster or shoulder holster. Most people aren't so fortunate, and even if you are, dry fire practice will make your draw much more efficient, smooth, and fast.

This is a very important skill to practice with dry fire because of the likelihood that you'll end up with a cover garment pulling your trigger as you reholster. It's also extremely likely that you may point the firearm at yourself at some point during your presentation.

I practice dry fire from concealment at my office 3-5 times a week with whatever I happen to be wearing at the time. It's important that you practice this with as much of your wardrobe as possible so you can see which techniques will work best with all of your clothes. As an example, my shirts clear differently based on how heavy they are, how long they are, and how tight they are. I've developed a one handed stroke to clear my cover garment, clear my holster, and present my firearm with the clothing that I wear on a daily basis. Most importantly, I test and confirm that it works hundreds of times a month.

Personally, I carry on my strong side hip, inside the waistband. What I do is draw my hand back along my body, clearing any cover garments, if I'm wearing one. Next, I hook my thumb up under my shirt(s) behind the butt of my firearm, move my hand forward over my firearm, and push my hand down as I grip the firearm and then pull it clear of the holster. The downward "push" helps me get a consistent grip on the firearm, and the muscle memory is transferrable when I'm carrying in a Serpa holster, which requires a downward push to release the retention.

Sometimes my shirt tail or coat gets stuck between my hand and the grip on my sidearm and I've found that I can push the firearm forward to remove the shirt. As a note, if there's any chance that your shirt could get inside your trigger guard as you re-holster with your method of carry, you need to figure out another technique for re-holstering. All of my holsters cover my trigger and thousands of dry fire repetitions have proven to me that this is a safe and effective option for me. It may not be for you.

Your draw stroke is going to be somewhat different depending on how you carry. In waist band (un-tucked), in waist band (tucked), 3:00 carry, appendix carry, crotch carry, cross draw, compression shirt, belly band, ankle holster, shoulder rig, purse carry, and in the pocket all require slightly different techniques, but here are the common elements:

1. Clear your cover garment.

2. Acquire your grip.

3. Clear your holster and continue with the 3 part draw stroke.

If you intend to carry concealed, go through the following sequence 10 times:

Clear your cover garment, Grip, Position 2, Safety off, Position 3, Trigger press, Rack the slide, Position 2, Safety on, Holster (This simply adds clearing your garment to the previous sequence.)

Here are 8 additional dry fire drills that you should do if you intend on eventually using the skills with live fire.

1. Emergency and tactical reloads.

2. Malfunction drills.

3. Single handed reloads (using your primary and secondary hand...both emergency and tactical). You can use your holster, waistband, pocket, or knees to hold the firearm while you're changing magazines and Dustin shows how to rack your slide one handed using your holster, belt, pocket, and knees (*figure 14*).

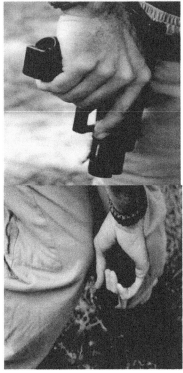

(figure 14)

4. Drawing and firing with the gloves that you normally wear (if you're in a cold climate)

5. Drawing and firing with your coat on. You may very well determine that your draw from under your coat takes so long that your only reasonable action is to find cover before attempting it. If this is the case, incorporate finding cover into your dry fire practice.

6. Drawing and firing after being knocked down (lay on the ground and practice drawing, aiming and firing from all orientations.) I've even started scenarios laying on the ground with a door laying on top of me to simulate someone kicking a door in/down.

7. Drawing and possibly firing while moving for cover. Don't move extra slow, simply so that you can fire a shot before you get to

www.TacticalFirearmsTrainingSecrets.com

cover. If you need to get to cover, get to cover...if you have time to shoot before you get there, fine. If not, get to cover and then pop out to shoot around your cover.

8. Work with a flashlight. Including identifying targets, acquiring your sights in the dark, keeping your support arm out of the line of fire and out of the way of the slide, as well as knowing what in the heck to do with the flashlight during malfunctions, and reloads (*figure 15*).

(*figure 15*)

9. Draw and aim your firearm while in your garage, sitting in your car. It should be obvious, but do not do this if there's a possibility that your neighbors will see you. And here are some advanced drills that you can do:

   1. Put your hands in ice water, snow, or salty ice water for as long as you can take it...30 seconds if you have arthritis up to 2 minutes, and then go through the same drills. It's your choice on whether to dry your hands off or not.

   2. Do calisthenics/workout until you're out of breath and then do your drills. If you notice that you're a little shaky and your fine motor skills aren't working quite right, that is the perfect time to train. Go through your drills then. You won't be able to simulate the exact fight or flight response, but you can inoculate your brain to many aspects of it by doing

firearms training when you are out of breath and or when your muscles aren't responding the way you expect. This may cause you to simplify your techniques considerably.

3. Video tape your technique and analyze it. Most new digital cameras have a video feature that you can use for this, or you can even use a $10-$20 web cam if the frame rate is smooth enough. As you analyze yourself, look for wasted motion. Try going through your drills at $1/2$ speed and playing back at 2x speed.

4. Practice malfunction drills with snap caps. (plastic shells that are the same size as real ammo that will cycle through your firearm) Practice failure to return to battery, slide lock malfunction, double feeds, and stovepipes if you're using a 1911.

5. With a partner, have them stand to the side while you press the trigger. While remaining aimed at the target, have your partner grab the slide of your gun and forcibly rack it backwards with approximately the same force as you'd get with a real discharge. Practice trigger reset by keeping the trigger depressed as you manage the recoil, reacquire your sights, and then let the trigger out until you feel the trigger reset. If you have snap caps, you can also do malfunction drills and reloads using this technique.

6. Dry fire training time is also the perfect time to practice keeping your sights on target while moving. The most accurate description that I've seen for this technique is calling it a "duck walk." In short, stand like you're going to start walking forward, drop your center of gravity about 6 inches and then move forward keeping your waist at exactly the same height. Put another way, bend your knees so that your belt buckle drops 6 inches and then keep it at that height as you walk.

You'll want to be squatted down as far, or further, than Dustin is in this example (*figure 16*):

(*figure 16*)

Imagine that you've got a rail running through your belly button towards your target that is straight as an arrow. The rail doesn't go up or down or right or left...it simply goes straight and your belly button needs to stay on the rail as you're moving forward..

This will give you a stable, consistent shooting platform so that you can aim, make accurate follow-up shots, and even make precision shots with enough practice while moving.

Another way to practice your duck walk is to do it while holding a video camera instead of your firearm. Ideally, your technique will be so smooth that your video looks like you're simply zooming in with no bounce or waving back and forth. You can practice it going forward, backwards, side to side, or even going up & down stairs.

Next, we'll cover using airsoft to put your dry fire training on steroids!

For questions and additional information, please go to
TacticalFirearmsTrainingSecrets.com/bonus

Airsoft...AKA Dry Fire on Steroids.

There is a lot of debate on the topic of using airsoft for firearms training. Most of the critics are simply professional fault finders who focus on a few shortcomings that they've seen with recreational airsoft and think that it applies to all airsoft training.

Other critics are people who are fortunate enough to have a job or the financial resources to allow them to shoot tens of thousands of rounds of live ammo per year, but these critics are normally won over quite quickly when they realize that airsoft is an enhanced version of dry fire rather than a substitute for live fire. In fact, I've been in my local airsoft supply store when a state law enforcement agency was picking up a case of spare Glock airsoft mags to go along with their case of Glock airsoft trainers.

So, I'm going to address this head on and tell you the top 6 problems people have with using airsoft for training and why they don't apply to you. Then I'm going to show you airsoft training in a whole new light and introduce you to some GREAT at-home training that you can start doing with airsoft.

I've got to start off with a safety warning. Treat airsoft trainers like real guns loaded with live ammo. The main reason to do this is to develop and maintain good firearms discipline. The second reason is that airsoft bullets have enough kinetic energy to break skin, go through your cheek into your mouth, and completely destroy an eye. This means always wearing safety eyewear when shooting and not pointing them at anything you don't want to destroy.

TOP 6 PROBLEMS WITH AIRSOFT TRAINING

1. **They're cheap plastic toys.** There are two broad categories of airsoft. Toys, and Training Pistols. You'll find the toys in discount stores and some sporting goods stores. They're usually clear plastic, light weight, fragile, inexpensive, and inaccurate.

The training pistols, sometimes called Professional Training Pistols or PTPs. PTPs are the same size and weight as their real counterpart...to the degree that good PTPs will fit in the same leather or kydex holsters as your real firearms. The controls are the same. They break down the same way. They don't have hoses coming out of them or any funky attachments sticking out (*figure 17*).

(figure 17)

The magazines hold both a small propane gas cylinder and plastic 6mm bbs. The propane gas cylinders propel the bbs and throw the slide back to provide recoil.

The trainer rifles have accessory rails that you can put your real optics on for training. Since most of the rifles have a 300-600 round per minute "full-auto" option, they use electricity from a lithium battery instead of gas to propel the bullet.

These training airsoft firearms look so real that if you brandished one in public, you should fully expect to get shot.

The solution to this "problem" is to get high quality, metal airsoft trainer replicas of one or more of the firearms you own.

2. **Lack of recoil.** High end airsoft guns DO have recoil, but it does not compare to a real firearm. There is no doubt that this is an accurate criticism...but it's also a GREAT benefit. One of the most common problems with handgun shooters is anticipating recoil. Basically, the brain decides that it knows how much the muzzle is going to rise after each shot and tries to compensate by pushing the muzzle down that much as you're shooting. The problem is that the timing seldom works right and the end result is low, inaccurate groups.

When you do training with airsoft, you don't have very much recoil and you train the brain to keep pointing the sights at your target all the way through your shot and reacquire them quickly after each shot. Since there's so little recoil to push the muzzle off target, you know immediately that any deviation in aim is because of something you're doing and you have the opportunity to quickly correct the problem.

This is especially helpful with new shooters or when teaching experienced shooters new techniques. By taking the feeling, sound, and shockwave of live rounds out of the equation, it allows the shooter to focus on their technique and not on the shock, euphoric feeling, or muscle fatigue that you get from firing live ammunition.

One of the problems that the lack of recoil DOES cause is that it messes with the cadence and rhythm that speed shooters have when practicing multiple shots in rapid succession. This IS valid, but doesn't really apply to very many shooters. Most shooters would benefit greatly from thousands of repetitions of smoothly clearing their cover garment, acquiring a solid, consistent grip, presenting their firearm, QUICKLY acquiring their sights and smoothly squeezing off the first shot. And, even competition shooters can and do use airsoft to practice everything up to double taps.

While you can't accurately practice double taps, you can practice follow-through by reacquiring your sights after each shot. In addition, what I do is set up two targets, 20 feet away from me and about 10 feet apart from each other. The practice that I get transitioning from target to target carries over very well to live fire...and this is something that my local ranges won't let me do outside of competitions.

One last note on the topic of recoil. .22 caliber barrels & uppers have gotten quite popular in recent years for 1911s, Glocks, AR-15s, and other firearms. I own a couple and LOVE them. As you can imagine, when you shoot your normal firearm with .22 rounds, you don't get nearly as much recoil or muzzle rise. The .22 inserts still provide a valuable training aid and help shooters put thousands more rounds downrange than they would otherwise. Is the recoil exactly the same? No. Can you still practice the fundamentals? Absolutely...just like you can with airsoft.

3. **Excessive magazine capacity.** I really get a kick out of people who have this "problem" with airsoft training. It goes something like this, "You can't do serious training with airsoft because they hold so many more rounds than a real firearm." Well, this "problem" requires a MOTO (master of the obvious) solution...when your training would benefit from realistic magazine capacities; don't load them up all the way. If you load 7 or 28 rounds in your real magazine, load 7 or 28 rounds in your airsoft magazine.

This isn't really an issue at all. If I'm training my draw stroke, I load the magazine all the way. If I'm training reloads, I only load 2-4 rounds in each magazine, whether I'm training with airsoft or live ammo. Even when training force on force...whether it's with airsoft, simunitions, or paintball, I load as few rounds as possible so that the interactions don't decay into a game.

4. **Trigger work.** The trigger pull and trigger reset on airsoft trainers are different than on real firearms, but they're also different between real firearms. Airsoft trainers still reward solid fundamentals. Press the trigger straight back and you'll get

tighter groups than if you over grip, pull with your trigger finger, or jerk the trigger.

Eliminate overtravel and start your trigger press as soon as the trigger resets, and you'll shoot quicker and more accurately, regardless of the firearm. These fundamental truths apply to both airsoft and live fire. You won't be able to practice the EXACT squeeze or the EXACT reset that you have with your real firearm, but you will be able to practice the fundamentals.

5. **Magazine changes.** With a real firearm, the magazine gets lighter as you shoot it and when your magazine is empty, it weighs a lot less than when it's full. This is very different with an airsoft pistol mag. Airsoft pistol magazines have a gas reservoir in them, as well as the bbs and are a big part of the weight of the gun. Since the bbs are only a fraction of a gram apiece, the magazines are almost as heavy when they're empty as when they're full. This wouldn't be a BIG problem, except that on almost all airsoft magazines, the feeder lips and the baseplate are both plastic and can break.

When you drop an empty airsoft pistol mag, you need to be a lot more careful than when you drop an empty real pistol mag... especially on concrete, tile, or other hard surfaces. Since the baseplate and the lips of the mags are plastic, they can and do break if they're dropped on hard surfaces.

There are three things that you can do to get over this shortcoming. The first is to position foam memory pad, a heavy blanket, a sleeping bag, or even remnant carpet strips wherever you plan on dropping your mags if you're training on a hard surface. The second option, if you don't have access to anything soft, is to do tactical reloads and retain your partial mags instead of doing emergency reloads and dropping your mags. The third is to use a drop bag on your belt and practice pulling your mags from your mag well and putting them in the drop bag. (This is standard operating procedure for many deployed units) None of these are perfect solutions, but they are workable.

6. **People who play airsoft.** Airsoft is a popular sport around the world. People who play it seriously dress up like military/SWAT (some are/were military or SWAT) and run scenarios against other teams, much like you would with paintball, laser tag, or like what our armed forces does with the MILES system. Some people take it as a game and view it like an adult version of "cops and robbers" and others use it as a serious form of force on force training. In fact, more and more law enforcement and military units are turning to airsoft as a training aid because of the extreme low cost of training.

But there are people who play airsoft who blur the line between reality and not-reality in their mind and talk like they've actually been in combat. Law enforcement door kickers who have been in live fire situations and combat veterans who have been there and done that hear these airsofters talk and get turned off by the entire method of training. This is a case where you should judge the training based on the facts and not on who else uses it.

In addition to the reasons I gave why these arguments don't apply to you, perhaps the simplest way to look at airsoft training is not to look at it as a substitution for live fire, but as a really fun and effective way to do dry fire drills, as well as some training drills that you just can't do with dry fire.

What's that mean? It means that neither dry fire or airsoft training shouldn't be viewed as a complete replacement for live training and that you should always follow up your dry fire and airsoft training with live fire. Some people suggest a 50/50 mix, while others suggest that you can make rapid improvements with 90% dry fire/airsoft and 10% live fire. In truth, don't get too hung up on the ratios.

Do as much dry fire and airsoft training as you can and you'll start seeing your live fire performance rapidly improving. Personally, I shoot 50-200 rounds of airsoft per day (integrated into my workout), dry fire a couple hundred rounds per week, and live fire a few hundred rounds per month on my own plus formal training and events.

Airsoft training is a case where perfect is the enemy of good. It could be easily argued that perfect training would be all live fire. Few elite forces would agree with you, but many competitive shooters make that argument. In any case, few people can afford the time and money required to do the repetitions necessary to lock in and maintain muscle memory with JUST live fire.

Keep in mind that the time you spend training with airsoft will ALWAYS be superior to the time that you *wanted* to spend training live fire but didn't actually do it because something got in the way.

One of the most famous anecdotes about using airsoft to train for live fire shooting comes from 2004 when Tatsuya Sakai won the US Steel Challenge. He couldn't legally train with a real firearm in Japan, so he trained with an airsoft gun for one year before the event. He came to the US one month in advance and trained with a real firearm to get his timing figured out and went on to win by beating some of the best names in shooting...guys who'd been training with 50,000-100,000 rounds of live ammo per year for several years.

I don't suggest that you only go out and shoot your real firearms once a year, but the time may come where that is more of a necessity than simply an option due to ammunition costs or restrictions on firearms. In the meantime, the benefits of cost, frequency of training, and the ability to train "prohibited" techniques makes it hard to beat airsoft training.

Let's take a look at the cost to shoot airsoft. I'm only going to figure the cost of ammo. I'll let you add in fuel, range fees, targets, and maintenance supplies. Let's compare 2 scenarios...one where someone buys 1000 rounds of ammo for their Glock and uses it at the range and another where the shooter buys an airsoft Glock AND shoots 100 rounds of live fire.

	Shooter A (live fire only)	Shooter B (airsoft and live fire)
1000 rounds of target 9mm	$250 (low ball)	
100 rounds of target 9mm		$30
NEW Airsoft Trainer Glock Pistol		$150

4000 rounds of premium BBs		$20
2 canisters of LP gas		$10
Airsoft Propane Adaptor		$20
Silicone Lubricant Spray		$5
Total spent for 1000 rounds	$250 with no rounds left to shoot.	$235 with 3100 rounds left to shoot.
Cost per round, when you only pay for ammo/ airsoft gas	25 cents per round	6/10ths of a cent per round

It's important to note here that the airsoft shooter in this example also shoots 100 rounds of live fire. Since the purpose of your airsoft training is to be able to perform better when you're doing live fire, it's vital that you practice occasionally with live fire. One of the biggest reasons for this is to convince your brain that your dry fire and airsoft training actually carries over to live fire so that when you find yourself under stress you'll not only have solid skills, you'll have already proven to yourself that you have solid skills.

But cost isn't the only benefit of airsoft training. When you use airsoft, your frequency of training will go up considerably. Think about it...all you have to do to shoot is throw a thick blanket or sleeping bag over a door, clip a target onto it with clothespins, make sure no animals or pets are around, put on your eye protection, and start shooting!

Here is a sample airsoft target setup using 20' of PVC, 4Ts, 2 elbows, 4 caps, a cheap tarp, and a moving blanket. These are the targets that I use because they're cheap at $30 apiece, adaptable, portable, and it's easy to replace individual components if they get shot when I use them for live fire (*figure 18*).

(figure 18)

When you're through shooting, simply throw away your target, run your vacuum to pick up the BBs, and you're done. If you place a container underneath, like I do, you don't even have that many BBs to pick up.

When it's that simple to shoot, you'll find yourself training 50100 repetitions, 3-7 days a week. It's MUCH easier to build up muscle memory this way than to blast through 500-1000 rounds every month or so.

"Prohibited Techniques." Airsoft will also allow you to practice techniques that are prohibited at most ranges like shooting while moving, shooting from behind cover, drawing from a shoulder or ankle holster, and shooting from and around a vehicle.

So, in addition to almost every drill that you can do with your firearm and dry fire practice, I'm going to tell you about some of my favorite at-home drills that airsoft guns are particularly suited for.

1. **Movement/Finding cover/shooting around cover/ concealment.**
   Gabe Suarez has trained shooters on force-on-force skills extensively with airsoft, paintball, and simunitions and one of the biggest factors that he's identified to increase your chances of surviving is to "get off the x" as soon as you realize "it's on." In other words, taking a stance, planting your feet solidly, drawing, aiming and firing isn't necessarily the best option, even though that's what how ranges force you to train.

   A better approach is that, instead of planting your feet, immediately start moving to cover or concealment as you're drawing your firearm. If you happen to be able to get a shot off before you reach cover, that's great. If not, get behind cover, get your firearm ready to go, and then decide whether to engage the target around your cover or retreat.

   This is a drill that is PERFECT for airsoft.

   [You can still put a hole in sheetrock, break windows and valuables, break skin, and rupture an eyeball, so you need to make sure that you're doing the drill in an appropriate area.]

   As an example, if you've got your target set up at the end of a hall, you can stand at the other end of the hall and instead of simply standing, drawing, and shooting, you can get your body out of the hallway as you're drawing and lean back into the hall to engage the target.

   You can also hit the deck behind a couch or bed and practice shooting around, over, and even under concealment. When I'm doing this drill, I'll usually wear knee pads so that I can hit the deck harder and faster than I normally would in repeated training.

2. **Punching and shooting.** It's been said that the main reason for handguns is to serve as a backup to a long gun or as a tool to help you fight to your long gun.

Well, there's another level to that line of thinking, and here it is. If you are within 21 feet of someone when a violent encounter happens, they will be able to get to you and hit/stab you as fast or faster than you will be able to get off your first shot. That, combined with the fact that most violent encounters will happen at "smelling distance" and not at 21 feet, it's quite possible that you'll have to use your hands to fight to get to your firearm/knife/OC or other weapon. In fact, recent National Institute of Justice studies of 10 years of law enforcement and civilian self defense shootings show that the majority of them happen within 11 feet.

I practice "fighting to my gun" in a couple of ways. I've got one of those "Bob" punching dummies that is a life sized torso of a man on top of a heavy, water filled base. I'll set it up next to a man-sized torso paper target to simulate multiple targets and I'll stand in front of the Bob and the paper target and assume that they have done something to start a violent encounter.

In this drill, I strike the Bob on the throat/neck/eyes/ears and then move away from "Bob" so that he is between me and the paper target as I draw my firearm...essentially slicing the pie and setting up a scenario where the untouched attacker has to go around his injured partner to get to me.

Then, I engage the punching dummy with my firearm and then slide to the side until I can see the paper target and engage it as well. (The airsoft BBs DO bounce/ricochet off of my punching dummy with a lot of speed and could hurt you or break things. There is also always a risk that the airsoft bbs will penetrate and permanently damage your punching bag/dummy. I usually have a t-shirt on my Bob and the airsoft rounds put holes in the shirt but my Bob is still 100% intact after taking thousands of rounds at close range.)

If your training environment permits and it won't cause alarm among neighbors, you can add in yelling commands, like, "Drop the weapon!"

3. **Transitioning from primary to secondary weapons.** This is a simple, but valuable drill if you ever carry both a longarm and sidearm...and another one that is hard for civilians to practice at ranges.

Put simply, the way I do this drill is to put 5-10 rounds in my airsoft M4 and go through drills. When my mag goes empty, I drop and retain it with my left hand and go for my sidearm and continue engaging the target. Anyone who has done this can tell you that this is easy to mess up on. Does your long gun even have a sling? Where does your long gun end up if you simply drop it? What do you need to do to make sure that you don't get caught up in your sling when drawing your secondary weapon? These are all problems that get flushed out with airsoft training.

My transition consists of pulling my M4 down and across my body with my left hand as I clear my holster with my right hand. Once I've cleared my long gun with my handgun, I bring up my left hand to assume a 2 handed grip (*figure 20*).

(figure 20)

4. **Transitioning from target to target.** If your local range prohibits shooting across lanes, you'll love being able to do this one. It's simple...set up 2 or more targets and engage them, one after another. I sometimes do this one with friends in my garage. I go out of the garage, they set up multiple targets, and I go into the garage and identify and engage them. To add to the difficulty, sometimes I'll enter the garage in the dark with my flashlight on strobe mode so that I have to maintain cover, identify targets, acquire my sights, and engage with the added disorientation of the strobe.

You can also do this with a headlamp strobe. These flash slower than a tactical flashlight strobe and, depending on the speed of your strobe, you might be able to do a drill where you identify and engage a target every time the strobe lights up. This version of the drill is simply fun.

5. While we're on the topic of shooting while in the garage, airsoft gives you a good opportunity to practice **drawing while in the drivers' seat of YOUR vehicle, practicing taking cover behind your engine block, and shooting around, over, and under your car**. Remember, you can break out windows, blind yourself or others, damage paint, and break valuables in your garage, so only do this if you are willing to take those risks.

   I do this drill several times a year, but the most important and most awkward time is in the fall when I change from summer clothes to winter clothes.

   When I started doing these drills around my car...the car that I paid for and didn't want to damage unnecessarily...I became VERY aware of the fact that it's possible to have a perfect sight picture of a target over the top of a car or other cover and still hit the hood of the car with your round. It sounds obvious, but since your barrel is lower than your sights, you need to raise your muzzle up over cover enough so that you don't shoot your cover instead of your target.

6. **Stress Drills**. Airsoft is also a great way to practice shooting when your fine motor skills aren't working right. While you can't completely replicate the stress response without stress, you can do some things to get used to manipulating your firearm when your hands and fingers don't respond as well as you'd like.

   The first drill that I do is to shoot during or after exercising. My normal workout is an interval workout where I go hard for 20 seconds and then take a 10 second break. During that 10 second break, I practice drawing my firearm and engaging targets. Sometimes I do it after a run, sometimes during/after doing a heavy bag or Bob workout. In any case, I wait until either; my heart rate is elevated, I'm shaky from an endorphin dump, or my hands don't work right from a post workout "pump."

   This is also a good chance to practice techniques to lower your heart rate quickly...namely combat breathing. Simply put, combat breathing is taking in a deep breath over a 4 count, holding it for a 4 count, and then breathing out through pursed lips for a 4 count. When you're breathing in, you want to focus on pushing your diaphragm down (stomach out) instead of pushing your chest up. This can quickly lower your pulse 10-20 beats per minute.

The second stress drill that I do is putting my hands in snow or ice water until they don't function right and then do airsoft drills. It feels like my fingers are sausages and like I'm wearing mittens, but this drill has helped me get rid of a lot of "fancy" gun handling techniques in favor of simple ones that are more likely to work under stress.

The third stress drill that I do is a completely different kind of stress, but still helps for training. It's going through drills using a shot timer. You can buy dedicated timers, or, if you have an iPhone, IPSC has a Shot Timer app that you can download for $10 and customize for however loud your particular airsoft gun is. When you go to the range, you can change the settings for live fire and you're good to go. Shot timers will record how long it takes you to get off your first shot and how long it takes between shots, providing measurable feedback on whether or not your skills are improving or not.

One of the drills I do with my shot timer is drawing from concealment while moving to cover. I hit the start button and a random countdown timer starts that takes from 2-3.5 seconds. When it goes off, I start moving towards cover and drawing/engaging my target or targets.

A second drill that I do is called "El Presidente." In one of it's most basic forms, it starts with the shooter looking away from a group of shoot and no-shoot targets. When the buzzer goes off, you turn around and engage all the shoot targets with one round to the center of mass and then one round to the central nervous system while not shooting the no-shoot targets.

And, a third drill that I do is to put 3-5 rounds in a mag and have a spare mag handy. I start the timer, draw and engage. When the slide locks back, I immediately reload, reacquire my sights, and re-engage my target. In this drill, I pay attention to my time to my first shot, but the focus is on the time between the last shot of my first mag and the first shot of my second mag. Basically, I'm trying to speed up the loop of identifying that my mag is empty, dropping the empty mag (or retaining it) loading a full mag, racking the slide (if necessary) and re-engaging my target.

You're on Camera! One of the biggest reasons to train with an instructor isn't so that they can teach you some incredible new "sexy" technique that will change your shooting overnight...it's so that they can identify and help you fix basic fundamental problems with your shooting.

At some point, you're probably going to know HOW to shoot with solid fundamentals better than you'll actually be able to shoot with good fundamentals. When you find yourself in this situation, pull out your video camera, digital camera with video, or web cam and start recording your airsoft training.

Doing this will allow you to quickly see if you are shooting with an aggressive stance like a fighter or if you're weight is on your heels; whether you're squeezing or slapping the trigger, whether you're reacquiring your sights as quickly as you should be, if you've got overtravel between shots, whether or not you're anticipating recoil, and where you've got wasted movement on your presentation, malfunction drills, and reloads.

If you have the ability to play back your recording at 1/2 speed or 2x speed, you'll pick up even more inefficiencies that you can improve.

As I mentioned before, don't be afraid to train at 1/2 speed...even with airsoft. It will allow you to imprint quality muscle memory and speed is one of the few components of your firearms handling that will increase when you're under stress.

Next, we're going to wrap things up by covering mental rehearsal and skill drills that will bring all of the training that we've covered together.

Mental Rehearsal—Secret weapon of Olympic Athletes, Special Operations warriors from around the globe, world class competitors, and YOU.

In the last 3 sections, we've covered the fundamentals of training, the importance of dry fire, and how to properly use airsoft as a turbocharged version of dry fire.

The next set of skills that we're going to cover may be the most important of all. You can do them in your car at stoplights, in bed as you're going to sleep at night, or even as a way to stay awake during a meeting at work. It's mental rehearsal.

When I say "mental rehearsal" I'm specifically talking about envisioning a situation where you are going to engage a target with your firearm and going through it in your mind from start to finish. This may include backing up parts of the sequence like you would rewind a video, repeating sections, and even visualizing yourself in the 3rd person and going through the motion and imagining what you would look like if you had a camera filming you from various angles.

In case you have any doubts about the value of mental training, I want to tell you about 4 groups of Soviet Olympians who competed in the 1980 Winter Olympics.

Group 1 spent 100% of their time doing physical training. Group 2 spent 75% of their time doing physical training and 25% doing mental training.

Group 3 spent 50% of their time doing physical training and 50% doing mental training.

Group 4 spent 25% of their time doing physical training and 75% doing mental training.

You can probably guess that group 4 did best by the simple fact that I'm including the story, but the amazing part is that group 3 did 2nd best and the group that did 100% physical training did WORST.

And then, shortly thereafter in 1983, a study was done at the University of North Carolina where basketball players improved their freethrow shooting ability by 7% by simply visualizing themselves using perfect form and hitting every shot.

These weren't isolated incidents. Since then, Olympic athletes, professional athletes, special operations teams, and SWAT teams have used mental rehearsal in combination with physical training to dramatically improve their performance over physical training alone.

In fact, a dramatic example of an Olympic athlete successfully using mental imagery is US diver Laura Wilkinson. Before the 2000 Olympics, Laura broke her leg and couldn't dive for several weeks while her leg was healing. Instead, every day she'd climb up on the 10 meter board, shut her eyes, and go through her routine in her mind. When her cast came off and she started diving again for real, she was at almost the exact same place in her training and won a gold medal in Sydney.

Elite athletes use mental imagery because at the top levels of athletics, almost everyone is equal in their talent and physical abilities. The big difference is how strong they are mentally, how few mistakes they make, how they're able to deal with adversity during competition, and how quickly they're able to identify and capitalize on their opponents weaknesses and mistakes.

You can take advantage of these same benefits of mental imagery, but there are some additional benefits that are particularly important for individuals training to use a firearm to defend themselves in a lethal force encounter. You'll quickly see other applications to martial arts training as well as almost any survival skill you can think of.

1. In an era of increasing regulation, mental training will always be legal...even in a Federal Building or on a plane.

2. As far as operational security and privacy goes, mental imagery will never give you away to your friends and neighbors as a gun owner or shooter.

3. Working through mistakes in mental training doesn't "cost" as much as mistakes do in real life.

4. It's free, fast, and you don't have to clean your firearm afterwards.

5. You never need to find a willing "victim" to play a violent attacker and do it exactly the way you want them to.

6. You're less likely to find obstacles to practicing a skill in your head than in real life. Bad weather doesn't matter, illness doesn't matter, traffic doesn't matter, and finances don't matter. The only obstacles for mental practice are internal.

7. Injuries don't happen when you do mental training.

8. Recovery times are shorter with mental training.

9. It is easier to practice perfect technique for 25 physical repetitions than it is to do 100 physical repetitions due to physical exhaustion. The remaining 75 repetitions that you do in your mind can be done to perfection because you have a clear image/memory of what the 25 perfect repetitions felt like.

10. You can do mental rehearsal while injured, sick, or separated from your firearm.

So, how do you do mental rehearsal? That's a million dollar question, and the answer can get as complicated and involved as you'd like, although I'm going to help you shortcut a lot of the learning process and tell you the techniques that will give you the biggest bang for the buck.

I'll give you some fundamentals that will help you quickly enjoy the major benefits of mental rehearsal. I say that because the topic of mental rehearsal gets incredibly involved once you move past the basic skills, and the marginal increase in effectiveness may mean the difference between silver and gold in

Olympic level competition, but most people will see incredible improvement by simply using the techniques that I'll share with you here.

Let's start by talking about sensory engagement.

That's a fancy way of saying that, as you're doing mental rehearsal, you want to think about what all 5 senses would be experiencing if you were doing physical training. One of the main reasons that you do this is to provide what's known as an "anchor" to your training. When you've repeatedly imagined a situation and then experience it, the more the actual experience matches up to what you've rehearsed in your brain, the more familiar it will seem. Your brain will basically say, "I've been here before. I've done this. I know how it goes and how it ends...and I know it ends well for me."

Here are some examples:

1. **What do you smell?** What does your firearm smell like before you shoot? How about after? When you're under stress, does your sweat smell different?

2. **What do you see?** How do your hands look wrapped around your firearm? As you're moving, does your sight picture bounce or stay smooth? What is in focus? Your front sight? How much space is on both sides of your front sight? What visual cues tell you that you should fire? What is your point of aim? A number on a target? The center of mass? Can you see what's happening inside your firearm as you pull the trigger as if you're looking at it with X-Ray vision?

   Do you have a full field of view, partial tunnel vision, or complete tunnel vision? Does your muzzle rise straight up or does it cant to the side as it recoils? Does fire come out of the end of your muzzle? How quickly do you reacquire your sight picture after each shot? Do you see heat waves coming off of your barrel as you fire more and more rounds? If you've got a 1911, what does a stovepipe look like and what do you do immediately when you see one? How is your sight picture different when your slide locks back on an empty mag and what do you do immediately?

Think about what your reloads look like. Think about what your malfunction drills look like.

Can you imagine being a cameraman and watching yourself from somewhere else in the room? (1/3 of Olympians view themselves from both first person (as you normally see things) and third person (like a camera on the wall, watching you.)) Do you have an aggressive stance? Is your stance stable? When you move, are you moving efficiently? When you clear and draw your firearm, is there any wasted movement? Are you shuffling your feet instead of crossing them?

3. **What do you taste?** Is your mouth wet or dry? Is your throat tight or dilated? Do you taste burnt gunpowder after you shoot?

4. **What do you feel?** What is each joint of each finger touching? How is your weight balanced? What is your breathing like? Can you feel yourself breathing with your diaphragm and your stomach going in and out? Can you feel your heart beat? Where do you feel it on your body? Can you feel your breathing and pulse rate slowing slightly and your field of view widening as you do combat breathing? How does it feel to draw your weapon? How is it different depending on your holster, clothing, and position? If you've got a retention holster, how does it feel to disengage the retention? If the retention doesn't disengage immediately, what do you do? If your firearm has a safety, how do you disengage it? How does the trigger feel as you bring up the slack? How about as the trigger breaks? How far back do you release the trigger before it resets? If the firearm doesn't go "bang," what do you do? If you're transitioning from one target to another, do you pivot at the shoulders, at the waist, or do you keep your entire upper body still and pivot using your legs?

5. **What do you hear?** What does your draw stroke sound like? If you have a safety, what does it sound like as it disengages? Can you "hear" anything as you pull the trigger? What does a good discharge sound like? What does the sound of your trigger resetting sound like? What does the sound of a malfunction

sound like and what do you do immediately when you hear this? What does the sound of your slide locking back after shooting the last round of a magazine sound like and what do you do immediately? What does it sound like when your firing pin drops on a bad primer and what do you do immediately?

How important are these drills? VERY important if you want to improve your firearms performance. Especially when you realize that your firearm is simply a tool and that your biggest weapon is your brain. The more you train your brain, the better it will be able to use the tools you have in your hands. These drills will help you improve your skills rapidly while saving you HUNDREDS of hours of range time and THOUSANDS of dollars in ammo and range fees.

OODA Loops

OODA Loop stands for Observe, Orient, Decide, Act, and the concept was formalized during the Vietnam War for fighter pilots. Between WWII and Vietnam, our Air Force became sloppy, relying more on the superiority of our jets than the skills of our pilots, and it cost us lives.

With the increasing speed of the jets in combat, the victor in air to air engagements was usually the pilot who could observe what was going on, filter it through their "orientation" or preconceived thoughts, decide on a course of action, and act the quickest.

Everyone in every confrontation goes through these four steps before taking action, whether it is a conscious process or not. The trick is to try to do it enough quicker than your opponent that by the time they have decided what to do, you have already acted and are no longer where they expect you to be.

By doing mental rehearsal, you can train your brain to identify threats and opportunities quickly. You can also train your brain to know that the situation is survivable and that you will be victorious. By running through several options in mental rehearsal and pre-deciding on the best course of action ahead of time, when the real situation comes, you won't have to waste time making decisions under stress...you'll just replay a script that you've already run in your mind.

The end result is that with proper mental rehearsal, you'll quickly go through your OODA loop and be taking action while other people are still standing flat footed with their mouths agape.

Mental Rehearsal for Self Defense

As we talked about earlier, many people reading this will be using mental rehearsal specifically to train for using a firearm for self defense. Obviously, shooting someone in self defense is not something that you can train at full speed or even half-speed. You CAN train for it with simunitions, lasers, airsoft, or paintball, but in order to do it effectively, you really need to train your brain for what is likely to happen in a firearms incident so that it won't surprise you when it happens.

One of the first things that is important to realize is that if you get shot with a firearm or are forced to shoot someone with a firearm, there is a 93-97% chance of surviving a gunshot wound. In TV and the movies, people die quickly and quietly after the first shot. The real world isn't so quick or clean.

When you're going through your mental rehearsal for self-defense scenarios, you need to keep this in mind. You might even want to run through scenarios in your head where you DO get shot/cut/hit and visualize yourself fighting through it and STILL eliminating the threat and being able to go home that night.

I go so far as to run through scenarios where I am out with my wife and sons and one of them gets shot. In these scenarios, instead of focusing on tending to them and eliminating their last line of defense (me), I run that 93-97% stat through my mind and immediately take out the threat and then tend to any injuries. It should go without saying, but I ALWAYS train successful outcomes.

Will this always work? No. One famous example of not being able to separate tragedy from performance was when US Olympic speed skater, Dan Jansen, fell in the 1988 Winter Olympics after his sister died. But an example of mental training paying off happened right before the 2003 Pan Am Games when US Pentathlete Anita Allen lost her best friend in Iraq. She was devastated, but went on to win gold and qualify for the Olympics. Again, it may not ALWAYS work, but you hopefully won't need it to work more than once in your lifetime.

At a minimum, you want to make sure that as you're running through scenarios in your mind where you're eliminating lethal threats, you envision the possibility that it will require multiple strikes or shots to stop your attacker. If the time ever comes where you have to use lethal force, you don't want to be surprised and stall unnecessarily when your first strike/shot doesn't stop your attacker. If the first shot stops the threat, that's great, but there's a good chance than it won't.

What Will You Say?

One of the benefits of mental rehearsal is that you can dialog with an attacker and have them say anything you want them to. You can also go through what you'll tell them:

"Drop your weapon NOW!" (instead of "Drop your gun NOW!")

"Lay face down and look away from me!"

"Cross Your Legs"

"Arms Straight Out"

What if They Comply?

A very difficult scenario for people who have only trained for lethal force encounters on a range or even doing force on force is what to do when your attacker actually listens to you. If you engage a home invader in your living room and you've got them laid out on the floor but your phone is in the kitchen and you're not sure if they're alone, what do you do?

Tase or pepper them to subdue them? Ask them to lay there like a nice home invader? Stomp on their ankle, wrist, or floating ribs? Strike them in the back of the head to subdue them? Cuff/plasticuff/zip tie them? If you decide to restrain them, what do you do first to insure that you don't end up in a wrestling match? Have THEM restrain themselves? The time to figure this out is during your mental rehearsal...not when your life depends on it.

What if you're a woman, you're out in public, and your phone is in the bottom of your purse? Can you get to it, unlock it, and dial 911 without taking your focus off of your attacker? Would you be better attacking them first, and then calling 911?

In any violent confrontation, what is your strategy for staying aware of your surroundings while you have your attacker laid out?

What If They Comply...partially?

One set of scenarios that you need to run through in your mind is what you will do if your attacker listens to your command to drop their weapon but then nonchalantly approaches you. Should you shoot them? Should you pull out pepper spray or a Taser and engage them? Keep in mind that if your attacker has intent to kill you, they may bet on you not shooting an unarmed person and walk right up to you. In other words, just because they've dropped their visible weapon doesn't mean they still can't rush you and kill you with their hands or your gun.

You also need to keep in mind that your attacker could change their mind at any point...if they detect that you have a weakness, that they have an advantage, or if they see a "friend" coming.

Mental Rehearsal for Combating Stress, Tunnel Vision, & the Shakes

Chances are good that you will get an adrenaline dump during a violent encounter or immediately afterwards and possibly before the police arrive. This is a VERY vulnerable time and you must stay switched on. In fact, as H. John Poole details in his excellent book, "Tactics of the Crescent Moon," Muslim armies have taken a page from Sun Tzu's tactics and have allowed their enemies false victories since the 7th century. In short, they know that there is a psychological letdown after a violent encounter from the medicine cabinet of hormones and brain chemicals that are released when someone thinks they've escaped death and won. To be fair, this tactic has been used to a certain extent by wise military commanders in every modern conflict... it's just much more effective, and less palatable, when a commander is willing to sacrifice the lives of the initial group of fighters to give their enemies a convincing sense of victory.

It's not uncommon for fighters to have a hard time staying awake in this state and many armies have purposely caused this effect by sacrificing small forces against enemy forces simply to get their enemy into this lulled state. Once their enemy's brains have started releasing their post-fight chemicals and hormones, the armies attack with their main force. It's smart and brutally effective as proven by a 1300+ year use of it.

If you find yourself in a lethal force encounter, regardless of whether your attacker listened to you or you had to subdue them in one way or another, you need to be aware of this chemical occurrence and stay alert and aware so that you don't slip into the vulnerable post-fight state too soon.

When you're practicing mental rehearsal, carry the scenario out in your mind until law enforcement arrives, you're a safe distance away, additional attackers attack, or friendly backup arrives.

Mental Rehearsal Routine of a Career Operator

When I interviewed internationally known firearms instructor, Randy Watt, he described his mental rehearsal routine. To put things into perspective, until recently, Randy was the Assistant Chief of Police in Ogden Utah. He's an internationally sought after SWAT instructor. He's a Colonel in the 19th Special Forces Group with multiple combat tours. AND, he's one of the elite few who have the critical combination of skill at arms and the ability to teach at a high enough level to be selected as an instructor at Gunsite.

Randy has decades of experience as a tactical operator and almost unlimited access to ammo and range time. Even so, Randy STILL uses dry fire and mental rehearsal. In fact, he considers them to be a vital component to his training.

Part of Randy's routine is the same, regardless of whether he is dry firing or on the live fire range. He'll start out with 5-10 minutes with his eyes closed, visualizing his body doing what it needs to do. The goal here is to bridge the gap between what the brain is focusing on doing and what the body is performing.

He goes further and breaks his presentation down into his component parts: Stance, grip, sight picture, sight alignment, breathing control, trigger press, follow through, and recovery.

This is similar to what Jeff Cooper, founder of Gunsite, taught when he told shooters that they could improve their shooting drastically by simply starting off their range time by doing 25 repetitions of getting a proper grip on their firearm. Even if that's the only part of your presentation that you focus on, everything that follows will improve.

Then next thing that Randy does is create an image around a situation that he is shooting. In other words, in his mind he isn't shooting at a paper target. He has created a situation in his mind and the paper target has turned into a 3 dimensional person who has entered the room where Randy is. The goal of this is to put the emotional component of a violent force encounter into static training.

This step helps a person make the jump from "shooting" to "training."

Randy does what good military, law enforcement, and other switched on people do and uses mental training in his daily life. As he's going up to his bank, he quickly games hold-up scenarios in his head so that he'll be able to react instantly if something happens. When he's with family and sees an unsavory character approaching, he games his response in his head. And when he approaches his home with his wife and puts his key in the door, he games potential threats that might be waiting for him on the other side.

He used these techniques as a member of SWAT, as a SWAT team leader, as a Special Forces door kicker, and as a Special Forces team leader. They worked and saved lives in those situations and it only makes sense to use them in everyday law enforcement and in off duty and civilian situations.

The more scenarios you game out in your head and the more often you do it, the deeper your response groove will be and the easier it will be for your brain to quickly pick an effective response in a crisis situation.

At this point, you appreciate the value of mental rehearsal, understand the most important fundamentals, and simply need a blueprint to follow. I'm going to start simple and build from there.

There are two major types of mental rehearsal that I do. Focused rehearsal and "current situation" rehearsal. I spend the most time doing focused rehearsal as I'm going to sleep at night, while waiting in line, or before shooting a stage for a competition. When I do focused rehearsal, I do several "repetitions" per session. I alternate between focusing on specific parts of my technique and the tactics of the situation. Sometimes it's all the same scenario, like before I shoot competitively, but I usually run several different scenarios in a row.

Current situation rehearsal is completely different and I do it throughout the day whenever I enter a new environment. It is focused more on tactics rather than technique. Here's an example. When I unlock my office and turn on the lights, I always game out what I would do if there was an attacker waiting. I take into account what I'm wearing, who's with me, what I'm carrying, and anything else unique to that day. The whole scenario takes from the time I remove my keys from my pocket until I turn the key in the lock—a couple of seconds at most—but it warms up my brain in case there actually is someone on the other side of the door.

So, here are a few specific mental rehearsal routines that you can do:

1. In bed before going to sleep, spend time going through the fundamentals of shooting--Stance, grip, sight picture, sight alignment, breathing control, trigger press, follow through, and recovery. Don't introduce a scenario at this time—just shoot targets. This should not cause your heart rate to increase or your breathing to change. Remember to involve all 5 senses and be as specific as possible with your mental pictures.

   Just like fundamentals should be the core of your live fire training, they should also be the core of your mental rehearsal. Run your drawstroke forwards & backwards in your mind, both as if you're looking out of your own eyes and as if you're watching yourself with a camera.

2. In bed before going to sleep, go through a few home invasion scenarios. How do you get out of bed? What do you grab first? If you have a lock/safe, what if it malfunctions? Can you tell if your firearm is in battery in the dark? Make sure you challenge and identify your home invaders as a legitimate threat...even during mental rehearsal. Sometimes you'll want to carry out the situation until police arrive. Sometimes you'll want to envision running into a relative. Other times, you'll want to envision finding everything's fine and confidently going back to bed.

If you find your heart rate starts going faster while you're doing this, it means that your mental rehearsal has enough detail that your brain is responding as if the situation is real. This is good for realism, but bad for sleeping. You can either use this as an opportunity to practice lowering your heart rate and blood pressure with combat breathing techniques, you can switch to mentally rehearsing fundamentals without scenarios, or you can stop running scenarios before going to sleep until you don't have as much of a response.

You'll find that the more you run through these scenarios in your mind, the more calm you become when you respond to "bumps in the night." Part of what you're doing is desensitizing your mind so that it doesn't over-release adrenaline if you actually do need to perform in a violent force encounter. So if you're having a hard time getting to sleep after running scenarios, start running the scenarios during the day until you don't have a psychological response to them. At first, you might even be able to mentally rehearse exciting scenarios as a tool to wake yourself up in the morning or when you're getting sluggish during the day.

3. Any time you're waiting in line, run through one or two situation specific scenarios.

4. When you're at a stoplight, run through one or two situation specific scenarios, taking into account your clothing, your seatbelt, your vehicle, and the vehicles around you. As a hint,

many times the best "solution" in these stoplight scenarios is to simply punch the gas, avoid confrontation, and escape.

Remember to always picture yourself walking away victorious. It's fine to imagine yourself getting shot, cut, or hit, but make sure that they don't affect your performance or the outcome.

Finally, we're going to tie all of the training methods that we've covered and go over a few specific regimens to help you get the most benefit out of the time you have for training.

For questions and additional information, please go to
TacticalFirearmsTrainingSecrets.com/bonus

Putting it all together

Over the course of this book, we've covered the quickest way to become a faster shooter, how to use dry fire to lock in firearms skills, using airsoft as a supercharged version of dry fire, and how to use the same mental rehearsal techniques that Olympic medalists use to become a better shooter.

In addition to saving money and time and helping you shoot better in the shortest amount of time possible, there are some additional benefits that preppers in particular will appreciate. First, in a time of increasing regulation and ammo shortages, one or more of these training methods will ALWAYS be legal. And second, in a SHTF scenario where you have to get people up to speed as quickly as possible while using as little ammunition as possible, these methods can't be beat.

Now, we're going to talk about how to put dry fire, airsoft, and mental rehearsal together into an organized training plan and I've got to start off with a well known quote, "Practice doesn't make perfect—Perfect practice makes perfect." Put simply, the strategies that I've covered will lock in muscle memory VERY quickly and it's important that you use them to lock in good technique rather than bad technique.

There are four training situations that we're going to cover: during a firearms class, after a firearms class, daily formal training, and daily informal training,

During and After Formal Training

The best way to lock in efficient technique is to start using these training strategies during or immediately after a training session with a firearms instructor. One of the ways that I do this is stay up on the line for an extra minute or so every time there's a break. I've never been to a group class where I could actually handle my firearm on the line during breaks, so I run through one or more of the following:

1. Practice the muscle motion of the technique we just covered with empty hands, eyes open.

2. Practice the muscle motion of the technique we just covered with empty hands, eyes closed.

3. Visualize myself running through the technique we just covered with perfect efficiency.

In one minute, I can run through a technique using any of the three strategies about 10 times or about 5 times if I break it down into components. These extra 5-10 perfect repetitions, several times during a class, can make a big difference. Remember, anytime you are learning a new skill you not only have to develop new muscle memory, but UNLEARN your old muscle memory. The more perfect repetitions you can run through in as short of a period as possible, the quicker you'll be able to lock in your new techniques.

As soon as you finish your class for the day, ask your instructor if you can stay a few minutes and run through some of the skills you learned with an empty firearm. There's few things more frustrating than teaching a class where the students don't take what you're telling them seriously so you'll usually find instructors will be very happy to let you run through dry fire drills on the range once they confirm that it's a cold range. If they don't want you to do dry fire on the range, then make sure to get somewhere where you can run through the techniques you learned as soon as possible...even if it's just sitting in your car with your eyes shut doing mental rehearsal.

Daily Formal Training

My training protocol is specific to my situation, which is defending against a lethal threat. My primary firearm is normally a handgun, and I usually carry concealed. When my primary firearm is my long gun, I open carry my handgun. The reason I say this is because you may need to add or change the specific skillsets that you practice from the ones that I use. As an example, if you're training for either cowboy action, the Bianchi Cup, IDPA, or IPSC, you'll want to add in specific sequences that you'll be using in competition.

I have an airsoft range set up in my office/warehouse area, so I train at least once a day and usually end up taking a couple of additional shooting breaks during the day. This is admittedly an ideal situation, and I haven't always had this option available. One alternative that I suggest is to set up a few targets in your garage and practice airsoft and/or dry fire every day when you get home from work—just make sure to ALWAYS remember proper safety protocols with both airsoft and dry fire.

One of the secrets to rapid improvement in firearms skills is how frequently and regularly you practice them. If you can run through 50 repetitions per day (a few minutes) for 20 days a month, you will not only have 1,000 repetitions per month, but since you're doing them every day, you won't lose any proficiency between sessions. Of course, if you can do 100-500 repetitions per day, that's even better.

Here's another way of looking at it. Let's say that your options are to do one of the following:

1. Run through 1,000 repetitions the 1st of every month.

2. Run through 50 repetitions every weekday of the month.

Let's say that the last day of the month is a Saturday and you need to use your firearm for real. If you did all of your training for the month on the 1st, then it would have been roughly 30 days since you last had trigger time. If you're spending a few minutes every day, then you would have had a little trigger time each of the last 5 days.

This is VERY similar to comparing someone who works out REALLY hard once a month to someone who works out a little bit every day. The person who works out a little bit every day will beat the once-a-month guy every time.

These are the skill sets that I train using a combination of airsoft and dry fire:

Drawstroke, (open/concealed) sight acquisition, trigger press, follow-through, reset.

Move to cover while drawing.

Transition from long gun to handgun.

Failure drills.

Reloads

Support hand

Fight to your gun. Start with hand to hand and transition to my gun.

Unorthodox positions. Seated, laying down (all directions), rolling, recovery & getting to cover starting on the ground.

Low light

One other thing that I've covered before, but that's worth repeating is that I usually combine calisthenics, heavy bag work, and weights with my dry fire and airsoft training. I do interval training where I workout for 20-60 seconds (wearing my firearm) and switch to firearms training during the rest periods. I'll repeat this cycle for my entire workout and really like the combination of high intensity physical activity and firearms training.

Here's an example training session from yesterday (all with my Glock in an in-waistband holster):

1. 4 sets of jumping lunges firing 3-6 rounds (airsoft handgun) between sets while drawing from concealment and moving side to side, changing mags when necessary.

2. 4 sets of kettlebell clean & presses engaging 2 targets with 3-6 rounds between sets while drawing from concealment and moving to cover, changing mags when necessary.

3. 4 sets of pushups firing 3-6 precision headshots between sets, changing mags when necessary.

4. 4 rounds on the heavy bag, firing 3-6 rounds at both the heavy bag and a paper target between sets, changing mags when necessary. (The purpose of this is to practice transitioning from fighting with my hands to fighting with my firearm.)

5. 10 SLOW dry fire repetitions of drawing, acquiring my sight picture, trigger press, and follow through with my sidearm.

6. 10 dry fire repetitions of drawing, acquiring my sight picture, trigger press, and follow through with my sidearm.

7. 10 dry fire repetitions of drawing, acquiring my sight picture, trigger press, and follow through with my sidearm, while moving to cover.

8. 39 SLOW dry fire repetitions of drawing, acquiring my sight picture, trigger press, follow through, (rack the slide) and repeat with my sidearm and snap caps. (39 rounds because I have 2 15 round mags and one 8+1 mag set aside for dry fire with snap caps.)

It's not that long...a couple hundred reps with different muscle groups, 50-100 rounds of airsoft, and 69 dry fire repetitions. The key is that if you do something similar every day, it adds up to thousands of repetitions per month. And don't worry about doing any specific exercise. I usually do additional sets of fighting-based calisthenics where the movements focus on the core and recovery after being knocked down, but you can do any kind of exercise you want or none at all.

You don't need airsoft to do any of these exercises, but most people find that they practice more often with airsoft than with just dry fire. If you decide not to train with airsoft and only use dry fire, I'm going to share something with you that I learned from author/shooter Steve Anderson in his book, "Refinement and Repetition: Dry Fire Drills for Dramatic Improvement" that changed the way I do dry fire.

When doing dry fire alone, Steve suggests, and I second, that you rack the slide for the first shot and then continue releasing and pressing the trigger for subsequent shots until you reholster. This lets you focus on acquiring and reacquiring your sights without being distracted by having to rack your slide between each shot to reset the trigger.

Remember, you can even run through these drills if you don't have your firearm with you by shutting your eyes and running through the drills in your mind. Don't underestimate the value of mental rehearsal. Your brain doesn't know the difference and repeated studies have shown that mental rehearsal is almost as good as—and sometimes better than—live practice, especially when it's used in combination with high quality live practice.

Every day, I run through slightly different drills. Some days I focus more on fundamentals, and some days I work on more advanced skills. Today, I'm going to be training with my AR-15 on a sling and my 1911 in a Serpa belt holster. I'll be working on the following:

1. React to a threat at different angles with my AR.

2. Left handed cornering with my AR.

3. AR mag changes.

4. Engaging multiple targets while moving to cover.

5. Transitioning from AR to 1911 and engaging instead of reloading.

6. Type 1-3 malfunctions with dry fire and snap caps.

If you use airsoft for training, I STRONGLY suggest that you follow-up your training sessions with a little dry fire time using your real firearm. You'll benefit from handling your firearm on a regular basis and knowing the feel of the trigger, but there's an even bigger reason. One of the biggest factors in how successful you'll be with your firearm under stress is your belief level in your skills. If you train primarily with airsoft and don't convince your brain that the training carries over to your real firearms, then you won't have the confidence that you need under stress.

Daily Informal Training:

In addition to "formal" training, I also suggest that you incorporate mental rehearsal into your training by either running through drills or scenarios in your head throughout the day. I do this when I'm at stoplights, when I'm standing in line, and before I go to sleep at night.

Sometimes I run through specific drills like acquiring my sights, reloads, or failure drills, but usually I run through scenarios like what I'd do if I was suddenly involved in a carjacking, holdup, or home invasion where I'm currently at wearing what I'm currently wearing and using whatever weapons I have available.

In my car, this involves visualizing what I'd do with my coat and seatbelt while drawing. In bed, it involves grabbing my light, getting my handgun out of my safe, evaluating triggers to decide if I have time to get my body armor, long gun, and tac vest, and the best way to keep my family safe.

For questions and additional information, please go to
TacticalFirearmsTrainingSecrets.com/bonus

In Conclusion

As we said in the opening of this book, these training techniques have been proven over several decades by elite units such as the US Navy Seals, Soviet and Russian Spetsnaz, GSG 9, British SAS, and US Army Special Forces, Detachment Delta, and Olympic gold medalists. They're used by professional and amateur competition shooters around the globe and, in many cases, they're the difference between first place and 5th or 6th place. Keep in mind that they don't use these techniques because of limited budgets—they use them because they're the absolute best training tools that they have available to them.

In short, they work and they work very very well if you will use them and we strongly encourage you to start doing so. At a minimum, start using mental rehearsal to run through drills and scenarios on a regular basis. You'll be pleasantly surprised at the impact that it has on your shooting.

Make sure to let me know the effect that these strategies have on your firearms proficiency (or other skills) by sending us an email at David@SurviveInPlace.com or Ox@OxTactical.com

Appendix 1. Maximizing Your Performance Under Stress

Ox here, co-creator of Dry Fire Training Cards and silent co-author of this book.

Due to the nature of this book, it's title, and our audience, we believe it's important to address some of the psychological and physiological components of performing at a high level in high stress situations.

It could be reacting to a family member having a life threatening emergency, responding to a natural or manmade disaster, stopping a lethal force threat, or everyday life challenges.

Through the years, I've encountered high stress situations where I've frozen with indecision. Fortunately, I have always "snapped out of it" quickly and taken positive action. I haven't always made perfect decisions—everyone makes mistakes that are easy to see with the eyes of a Monday morning quarterback—but I've made mostly good decisions.

But this has led me to dig into why some people freeze under stress, some people make bad decisions under stress, and some people thrive under stress.

When learning to drive, I wondered how I'd handle different emergency situations. When learning to fight, I wondered how I'd handle different surprise attacks at full speed. When learning medical skills, I wondered how I'd handle someone with a critical injury. When learning combative shooting, I wondered how I'd handle myself in a gunfight. You're probably the same way. You always wonder how you'll perform "when it counts" until after the first time it actually does...then you'll wonder how you can do it better the next time.

It's important to ask why different people with the same training, using the same technique, perform SO differently when the fit hits the shan? Traditional wisdom says that your fine and complex motor skills will disappear under extreme stress, but personal experience and the experience of many people that I've known and people I've studied have shown me that it's not a black/white, all/nothing issue.

This has been top-of-mind for me lately as I've dealt with several rabid "haters" who say that using the slide stop on a pistol during a tactical reload is a fine motor skill and will always fail under extreme stress. I have too many friends who have been in combat who have made it work, and this led me to dig into why some people can do fine motor skills and complex motor skills under stress and others can't.

There's a saying that "In a life or death situation, you won't rise to the occasion…you'll perform at half the level that you do in training." But that's not always true. Some people DO rise to the occasion. They're "clutch players." They're unflappable and perform no matter what. The question becomes, what factors dictate high stress performance and how can we control them and use them to our advantage?

The following is a work in progress and open to input, but it is an equation that attempts to quantify what is needed to perform under extreme stress:

$$\text{Performance} = (\text{inoculation} + \text{state control} + \text{fitness level}) \times (\text{familiarity} + \text{myelination}) \times (\text{comfort with unknown} + \text{decision making})$$

If math's not your thing and your brain just froze, keep reading…in simplest terms, the better each of these factors are, the better you'll perform under stress.

At the risk of turning this into a book, I'm going to cover each of these briefly. I encourage you to self-assess in each of these areas and see how you can increase the chances that you will perform at a high level under stress.

A point of note to the vast majority who aren't math nerds. Each group of factors within parentheses are related. Theoretically, as long as at least one of them is not zero, you'll be able to perform the skill to some degree under stress. This is not hard-and-fast and I covet input on how to refine it.

With that, let's get into each of the factors:

Successful past stress inoculation: Simply put, you'll perform better in situations that you've been in before. I find that, in shooting defined stages or courses of fire, I perform 20-30% faster the 2nd time I shoot the course of fire than the first time. I noticed the same phenomenon in sports, fighting, dealing with emergency trauma and medical situations, driving emergencies, and more and I'm betting that you can think of several personal examples from your own life.

On lethal force encounters in particular, Ken Murray, co-founder of Simunitions, has found that officers and soldiers are working out the kinks until about the 3rd successful and justified lethal force encounter. That being said, the ramp-up is much faster and easier for someone who has been gradually exposed to stress inoculation while mastering their craft than someone who has done all of their practice in a stress free environment.

Retired Navy SEAL, Larry Yatch, has had similar findings. He's found that, in general, stress shooting performance is maximized with a mix of 80% dry fire, 10% live fire, and 10% force on force with simunition, UTM, or paint ball training.

Regardless of the situation, the more successful exposures you've had to similar situations, the lower your heart rate will be, the less adrenaline and cortisol your body will release, the clearer your thinking, and the more in control you'll be the next time you're in a similar situation.

I recently heard an officer talking about his first lethal force encounter. One of the comments that he made was that it wasn't *really* the first time that he successfully stopped a lethal threat with a firearm. He'd mentally rehearsed the scenario hundreds of times before and nothing about the scenario surprised him when it was happening in real life.

Next is **State Control**, which is worthy of it's own chapter or book. I'm going to cover it briefly here. If you want more information on this, please contact me at ox@oxtactical.com or by going to http://1holegroup.com/

In short, I'm calling state control the ability to control the state of your mind in situations where others aren't or can't. When you can stay cool, calm, and collected and have ice running through your veins, you can perform at levels much closer to how you perform in practice than having everything fall apart. Is it easy? No. Is it possible? Absolutely…as evidenced by the feats that brain surgeons, neuro surgeons, trauma surgeons, combat medics, and warriors throughout the ages have been able to accomplish in "impossible" conditions.

Here's where the rubber meets the road. Let's say that you're violently surprised and have an adrenal response. The initial release of adrenaline, which you probably can't control, will happen subconsciously in less than 1/100th of a second. Someone without state control will keep releasing adrenaline…both draining their adrenals and seriously compromising their ability to perform fine and complex motor skills and perform higher level thinking. But someone who does have state control can quickly slow the flow of adrenaline. The quicker they do it, the more likely they'll have an optimal amount of adrenaline in their system that doesn't rob them of performance. Also, since adrenaline has a half-life of approximately 90 seconds, the quicker you stop the release, the quicker you'll be back to a "normal" state and the less of an "adrenaline hangover" you'll have.

The factors that I've identified that make up state control include the following:

Inner compass (which is complex, but for me includes my Christian beliefs, belief that my life is worth defending with whatever force is necessary to insure that my wife has a husband and my sons have a father at the end of the day, and belief that innocent people should be protected from evil people). Matt and Sherrie Seibert (1holegroup.com) have come up with the best process that I've ever seen to get people to internalize the fact that it's OK for good people to do bad things to bad people who are in the process of committing evil acts.

Nutrition, hydration, and sleep. Pretty self-explanatory. A deficiency in any of these makes it hard to respond to stress effectively and remain in control.

Brain chemistry and hormone levels. There's a lot of crossover here with nutrition, hydration, and sleep, but I feel that they're worth separating out. Ironically, when people's adrenals are fatigued, they're more likely to "go straight to 11" rather than having a measured response.

Unconscious mind/flow state/the zone. High performers and extreme athletes are all familiar with and constantly seek flow state and/or the zone. It's a state of mind where the unconscious mind does most of the driving, time appears to slow down, balls/hoops/targets seem to get bigger, the body relaxes, Alpha waves in the brain increase, creativity flourishes, and amazing things happen.

Next time you see a musician doing independent motions with their right and left hands AND right and left feet AND singing, this is what's going on. What they're doing is completely impossible to do consciously and must be driven unconsciously or by the subconscious mind.

For most people, this is a fleeting state that happens outside of their control without rhyme or reason. They think that some people "have it" and some don't. That's simply not true. This kind of performance is amazingly normal and you can trigger it on command and at will with the 1holegroup.com training.

Will Power, confidence. Again, there's a lot of crossover with these and other factors, but I'm pointing them out because they can be easily be influenced in yourself and in others.

Pain/injury level. This is a tough one to place in the equation. I view pain and injury somewhat differently than most. It's been incorporated into a few trainings and courses that friends of mine have put out, so you may be familiar with it already. In short, I view pain/injury as a constant that the mind acts like a lens on. The mind can use this lens to cause the pain/injury have more or less of an effect on mental and physical performance. There are definite limitations to this, but the discipline/skill of being able to minimize the effects of pain is very valuable.

One person can get a paper cut, see their own blood, and become completely frozen and ineffective. Another can be unfazed by life threatening wounds.

Pain and injury can be distracting and take mental resources away from performing a needed task at a high level in a stressful situation.

Fitness level. In general, the more fit a person is, the better they'll be able to deal with a stressful situation. Add to that the fact that if the stressful situation requires dynamic movement, the exertion will be less stressful if you're fit than if you're not.

Familiarity of the task at hand. Most people remember a time when they drove around a corner and their rear wheels lost traction. Instinct is to turn away from the skid, but the right move is almost always to turn the front wheels into (towards) the direction that you're skidding. The more times you're exposed to this situation and have successful outcomes, the quicker you'll respond and less stressful it will be in the future.

Thickness of the myelin sheaths around the neural pathways for the task at hand. This sounds more complicated than it is. Practice something over and over the same way and you'll develop neural pathways (muscle memory). Keep doing it and you'll develop a fatty (cholesterol) sheath around the neural pathways that partially insulate the neural pathway from the performance robbing effects of adrenaline and cortisol. In other words, practice something until it's boring and you'll be able to do it under stress better…regardless of whether it's a gross, fine, or complex motor skill. Why?

This is overly simplified, but it's like running a maze in the dark, blindfolded. If you've done it so few times that you have to think about the process, it's going to be a long and painful experience. But, if you've done it enough times… first slowly in the light, then speeding up, then gradually taking away the light…then you no longer have to consciously drive the process. The process is a conditioned response that you simply make the decision to start and the unconscious mind automatically fires off all of the neurons necessary to take you through the process and to the desired finish.

Comfort with the unknown and the ability to boldly make decisions. Also called "paralysis by analysis", these are factors that are hard to quantify, but I've definitely seen them play a role in performance under stress. Fortunately, once you make the choice to start looking for opportunities to improve in these areas, your mind will start spotting them—then it's just a matter of disciplining yourself to make educated choices when the outcome is stacked in your favor but not guaranteed.

Again, the equation I shared is not a hard and fast guideline and the factors I mentioned probably aren't the only ones to consider, but if you honestly assess yourself in each of these areas and pick one or two at a time to work on, you'll quickly see that your ability to react positively to stressful situations improves.

-Ox out.

Ox@OxTactical.com

Safety Warning!

Firearms are tools that give people the power to destroy at a distance. Firearms are inherently dangerous. Negligence and accidents can lead to permanent injuries, jail time, and possibly even death.

Treat every firearm as if it is loaded at all times, and don't point them at anything that you don't intend on destroying. Don't point them at a wall that may have something on the other side that you don't mind destroying. When you handle a firearm, YOU are responsible for everything that happens as a result, so get proper live training from a qualified instructor.

This book does not substitute for live training with a qualified instructor. It is meant to enhance and lock in the skills that you learn from live training. The author, publisher, editor, and talent for this book take no responsibility for what you do with firearms or what happens to you as a result of being around firearms.

If you don't think a particular activity is safe, or that you can safely do it, then don't do it.

Stay safe. Obey the law. Don't do careless things.

Sign up for additional firearms training for FREE!

As someone who has purchased this book, you are entitled to additional firearms training information for FREE by going to TacticalFirearmsTrainingSecrets. com/bonus.

While you're there, you'll be able to get additional training tips, interact with other shooters, and get priority notification about recommended training courses.

Made in the USA
Las Vegas, NV
30 August 2023